In Search of
Sir Richard Burton

Woodburytype photograph of Burton, originally published in *Men of Mark: A Gallery of Contemporary Portraits* (1876).

In Search of Sir Richard Burton

Papers from a Huntington Library Symposium

Edited by Alan H. Jutzi

Huntington Library
San Marino, California

© Copyright 1993 by the Henry E. Huntington Library and Art Gallery

Published by Henry E. Huntington Library and Art Gallery
1151 Oxford Road, San Marino, California 91108
All rights reserved.
No part of this book may be reproduced in any form or by any means, electronic or mechanical, including photocopying and recording, without permission in writing from the copyright holder.

Printed in the United States of America

In search of Sir Richard Burton: papers from a Huntington Library
    symposium / edited by Alan H. Jutzi.
        p. cm.
    Includes bibliographical references.
    1. Burton, Richard Francis, Sir, 1821-1890—Congresses.
    2. Explorers—Great Britain—Biography—Congresses. I. Jutzi,
    Alan H., 1945-
    G246.B8I5 1993
    910' .92—dc20
    [B]
                                                      93-16173
                                                         CIP
    ISBN 0-87328-140-3

To Edwards H. Metcalf

*longtime patron of the Huntington Library,
book collector extraordinaire, and Burton devotee*

Contributors

M. Guy Bishop, a specialist in Western American and Mormon history, has taught at the University of Southern California and several community colleges in the Los Angeles area. He has recently published articles in the *Journal of Mormon History, California History,* and the *Utah Historical Quarterly.* His book, *Mormon Footsoldier: The Life of Henry William Bigler, 1815-1900,* is forthcoming from the University of Utah Press.

Jim Casada is a professor of history at Winthrop University in South Carolina. He is the author of *Sir Richard F. Burton: A Biobibliographical Study* and several other books on African explorers. He has also written widely on sport in Africa and elsewhere.

Burke E. Casari is a longtime collector and researcher of Richard Burton. He first became interested in Burton while he was senior English lecturer at N'Jala Teacher Training College in Sierra Leone, West Africa, in 1962-63. Following his return to the U.S, he began gathering what has become a varied collection of books, journals, illustrations, letters, and other Burton materials.

John Hayman is a member of the Department of English at the University of Victoria in British Columbia. His publications include *John Ruskin and Switzerland, Robert Brown and the Vancouver Island Exploring Expedition,* and *Sir Richard Burton's Travels in Arabia and Africa: Four Lectures from a Huntington Library Manuscript.*

Alan H. Jutzi is curator of rare books at the Huntington Library.

Quentin Keynes, a filmmaker as well as a prominent book collector, owns a remarkable collection of Burtoniana. He lectures throughout the world on Africa and on Richard Burton.

Stephen Tabachnick, currently chair of the English Department at the University of Oklahoma, has also chaired the English departments of Ben-Gurion University of the Negev and Tennessee Technological University. He has been visiting professor at the Hebrew University, San Diego State University, and UCLA. His most recent publication is an article on the Anglo-Arabian traveler Wilfred Thesiger.

Donald A. Young is a professional African safari guide with a broad knowledge of East Africa and its history. He has studied Burton in depth, and for his 1979 master's thesis at the University of Nebraska he prepared "The Selected Correspondence of Sir Richard Burton, 1884-1890."

Table of Contents

Introduction. 1
   Alan H. Jutzi

The Letters of Capt. Sir Richard Burton:
New Sources on the Nile Controversy 5
   Donald A. Young

Burton as Autobiographer 27
   John Hayman

Burton's Review of Doughty's *Arabia Deserta* 47
   Stephen Tabachnick

"The Captain Has Seen Utah without Goggles":
The Mormons and Richard Burton 61
   M. Guy Bishop

Additions to Burton's Bibliography 71
   Burke E. Casari

Burton and His Library 85
   Alan H. Jutzi

The Labyrinthine Paths of Collecting Burton 107
   Quentin Keynes

Concluding Remarks 133
   Jim Casada

Introduction

Captain Sir Richard F. Burton, who became a legend in his own time without securing the full approbation that many believe he deserved, has perhaps finally received his due in this generation. There are no less than four biographies of Burton available here and in England. Edward Rice's 1990 publication was a runaway best-seller; Byron Farwell's creditable study, which first appeared in 1963, has been reprinted in paperback; F. J. McLynn's full-scale biography *Burton: Snow Upon the Desert* came out in 1990; and Fawn Brodie's *The Devil Drives* (1967), considered by many the best of the group, is readily obtainable in American libraries. To these printed studies must be added the 1989 feature film *Mountains of the Moon*, based largely on a fictionalized account of Burton's life.

Although Burton's current popularity can be traced in part to his adventures as an explorer, his pursuit of the forbidden, and the notoriety he himself fostered, there is a serious and continuing interest in the less exotic and more cerebral aspects of his career. As Frank Harris has pointed out, Burton was not only a man of action but an extraordinary scholar. He demonstrated both intellectual curiosity and discipline and made perceptive observations about whatever and whomever he encountered. But Burton was not a philosopher, and his candid statements played a role in advancing the appalling racial attitudes of the Victorians. Still he held a remarkably expansive view of the world's cultures, and it is perhaps Burton's infatuation with cultural diversity that late twentieth-century America finds most appealing.

On 19 and 20 October 1990, a group of scholars, book collectors, librarians, and those simply interested in Richard Burton met at the Huntington Library in San Marino, California, to listen to formal presentations as well as informal talks on Burton's life and writings. The conference was conceived by Edwards H. Metcalf, a longtime patron of the Huntington, who as a young man began collecting printed works and autograph Burton material, and who has wholeheartedly supported scholarly research in his collections. The purpose of the conference was to honor Burton, to reassess his achievements and look forward to future Burton projects.

The Huntington was indeed an appropriate location for the conference because Burton's own library of twenty-seven hundred books, pamphlets, maps, and documents came to the Library in 1986. This collection, neglected by Burton biographers, was purchased and deposited at the Huntington by the late Allen D. Christensen and the Christensen Fund of Palo Alto, California. Mr. Christensen's generosity created the largest Burton archive in the world.* Some of these items were displayed at the Library in 1988 in an exhibit entitled "Sir Richard F. Burton: Explorer of a Dozen Worlds." In 1990, the centennial of Burton's death, the Huntington sponsored not only the conference but the publication of *Sir Richard Burton's Travels in Arabia and Africa: Four Lectures from a Huntington Manuscript*, edited by John Hayman. These lectures, originally delivered by Burton in Brazil, provide an eminently readable introduction to his travels in Africa and the Middle East.

The success of the conference—the variety of the topics and quality of the presentations, and the new historical material that came to light—prompted the Huntington to publish the proceedings. The remarks of Quentin Keynes, one of England's prominent book collectors, demonstrate in particular the atmosphere that prevailed at the conference. He brought to the Library highlights from his marvelous Burton collection and spoke informally about its assemblage, value, and history. His talk and the discussion following were preserved on audio tape and then transcribed and edited, so that the reader gets a real sense of the vitality of his comments and the response of the audience.

The concluding remarks, by bibliographer and scholar Jim Casada, reinforced the shared belief of the participants that despite the numerous Burton biographies there was still much to be learned about this baffling and many-sided man. As Burton investigated the multiplicity of human customs so we attempt to understand his life and work—to identify and appreciate his varied contributions as an explorer and scholar. We hope that this volume of short studies contributes to that intriguing search.

Alan H. Jutzi
Huntington Library

---

* Throughout this volume, items in the Burton Library are identified with their number from B. J. Kirkpatrick's *A Catalogue of the Library of Sir Richard Burton* (1978).

El - hadj (the pilgrim) Abdullah

Photograph, ca. 1854, from the Edwards H. Metcalf Collection (Huntington Library).

The Letters of Capt. Sir Richard Burton: New Sources on the Nile Controversy

by Donald A. Young

I have always thought it a great irony that Sir Richard Burton remains one of the most mysterious figures of the nineteenth century. He wrote or translated some eighty books and over a hundred articles, traveled almost everywhere and spoke to people in twenty-nine different languages, and yet we know very little about him personally. We do know, of course, the story of his grieving widow Isabel, who burned his manuscripts, diaries, and journals—all the materials we would most like to have consulted. So it seems Burton is fated to remain an enigma.

The subject of this essay is an examination of an exciting source of information about Sir Richard Burton—his own letters. I have managed to track down, translate, and annotate over three hundred letters written between 1841 and 1890. The letters provide valuable insight that Isabel failed to destroy and that even Burton's most recent biographers have failed to consult. The Burton letters, relatively few in number compared to the letters of T. E. Lawrence, for example, illuminate the

---

Letters in the collection of the Royal Geographical Society and in the Houghton Collection, Trinity College Cambridge, are quoted by permission.

range of roles that Burton played, from the virile young adventurer of Arabia, to the Nile explorer, to the lonely and frustrated consul at Fernando Po, to the neglected savant of Trieste. The letters require few major revisions in what we already knew about Burton but, perhaps more importantly, they provide details about Burton's everyday life and chronicle his many interests and moods. It is tempting for us, in view of Burton's accomplishments, to regard him as a man of innate and effortless brilliance, but when we actually read letters describing his day-to-day labors over a period of thirty-five years, we realize what dedication, self-discipline, and hard work made his achievements possible.

In his letters Burton directly addresses some of the matters that have involved historians and biographers in fruitless speculation; I believe it is time to let Burton speak for himself, on such questions as race, sex and erotica, his relation to the Royal Geographical Society; and above all, on the sources of the Nile. Below are a few excerpts from the letters; the source of each follows in parentheses.

A letter written to Dr. Norton Shaw, assistant secretary of the Royal Geographical Society, just after the famous pilgrimage to Mecca, shows Burton at his most self-critical:

> My Dear Shaw,
> I've been laid up since writing to you—the usual dysentary [sic] which welcomes one on return from a hard trip. I won't say it was aggravated at my disgust at my failure in crossing the Peninsulas, but joking apart, the "physic" of a successful man differs wildly from that of the poor devil who has failed.

Later in the same letter Burton describes the thrill of a new flirtation.

> We've an American missionary woman at the Hotel who

proposes authorship: Tis to be hoped she won't write as she conversationalizes. As I'm still dressed [in disguise] and called the Haji, she funks me a few. But at dinner I see the case will open and consequently, Oh Shaw! wonderful are the tastes of Yernen which are conveyed to her "sensorium." (Burton to Shaw, 16 November 1855; Archives of the Royal Geographical Society; hereafter "RGS")

Burton was often a critical and caustic observer of native races, but he could also be appreciative, as in this letter to Monckton Milnes:

Those who talk of the benighted African should have seen the envoy who conveyed to the Governor the ultimatum of the Ashanti King. There was not a European on the coast to compare with him in dignity, self-possession and perfect savoir-faire touching the object of his mission. (Houghton Collection, Trinity College Cambridge; hereafter "TCC")

Here is an example of Burton at his cynical and wicked best:

I have been here three days and am generally disappointed. Not a man killed nor a fellow tortured. The canoe floating in blood is a myth of myths. Poor Hankey must still wait for his peau de femme. Not a slash have I been able to attend. At Benin au moins they crucified a fellow in honour of my coming—here nothing! And this is the bloodstained land of Dahome!! Disguested with the tameness of the place—the king will not be back for a month —I return this afternoon to Whydah on the coast and shall run about a little before getting back to Lagos. The yellow fever is so bad in the Bight of Biafra that I daren't take a cruzer there. So most probably, I shall go up the Niger and attempt Timbuktu in a canoe. Really it will be a curious spectacle for the immortal gods to look down upon, a chap starting up a river with an infinitesimal prospect of returning! I ask myself "Why?" and the only echo is "damned fool!" <u>Enfer</u> needs must where the Devil drives! (TCC)

On holiday in Britain in December 1864, Burton wrote to his vice consul, Frank Wilson:

> . . . all of my people are in the country doing their Xmas; occupations compel me to remain in town without other company than Lord Damndreary. The cold is awful, rain & frost, no snow yet. At the F.O. [Foreign Office] they had the impudence to congratulate me upon my return home. Speechless, I pointed out the window, through which appeared a pea-soup fog defiling the face of earth and heaven and when voice returned I faintly asked what they could mean; . . . it is already on the books that my stomach may be stuffed with plum pudding and already reproaches for not eating mince pies are being showered upon my head. After all, there are worse places than West Africa. (Quentin Keynes collection; hereafter "QK")

When Henry Stanley, the American journalist, first returned to England from his successful search for David Livingstone, he received the same cold treatment that Burton had from the R.G.S. Identifying a kindred spirit, Burton instantly took Stanley's side:

> Yesterday I interviewed Stanley. . . . I think him the right sort. The R.G.S. has, as usual, put its foot into the wrong hole. (Burton to Milnes, 23 September 1873; TCC)

Once resigned, at least temporarily, to the fact that his career as an explorer had been brought to an end, Burton poured all his energy into another interest, the translation of foreign literature into English. Burton wrote to Lord Houghton from Trieste:

You'll understand how hard I've worked when 8 volumes have been finished since Dec. 6, '72. By this time next year, 15 vols. will be ready—of course not printed at once. Perhaps if Bri. Pub. [the British public] had known this it might have insisted upon my being sent to Africa. (5 November 1873)

My broadsword exercise (quite new & my own invention) has been submitted to the Duke with his approval. I have offered my cavalry pistol gratis to the War Office. I have—never mind. (Burton to Milnes, 15 June 1875; TCC)

In spite of his constant activity at Trieste, he felt restless and caged:

You might suggest to Mr. Dis [Disraeli] that Trieste is not half large enough to hold me, but that I would be contented with Central Asia or even unknown Africa. (Burton to Milnes, March 1875; TCC)

With the private issue of his translation of the *Thousand Nights and a Night* in 1885, Burton received financial rewards such as he had gained from none of his other books. However, his literal and vivid translations from the Arabic with his own lively annotations alarmed such groups as the London Vigilance Society and other anti-pornography organizations, and consequently Burton spent his last years under the threat of fines and imprisonment. Undaunted, he continued with his crusade to introduce the English reading public to such books as the *Ananga Ranga* and the *Kama Sutra*. At sixty-eight years of age, suffering from gout, his body scarred by the ravages of a lifetime of travels in the wilds, he hurled defiance at his critics:

If I am brought into court it will be with the Bible and Shakespeare, and I will insist upon reading the passages at point. (Burton to Smithers, 9 August 1889; Henry E.

Huntington Library; hereafter "HL")
Burton had once written:

> When old I intend to take a permanent passage in some steamer & go round and round the world till I die. (Burton to Milnes, 29 August 1876; TCC)

Such had not been possible because financial worries and failing health compelled him not to stray far from Trieste. The letters written in the months prior to his death are filled with the details of his daily labors:

> Two day ago, I finished "final copy" of Catallus and have begun to polish it up—which will take some time. I will then copy it myself again, re-correct it and give it to my copyist at Trieste so that you may be spared the bother of decyphering me. (Burton to Smithers, 20 February 1890; HL)

> I am working too hard at <u>Scented Garden</u> for other disport and keep <u>Ausonius</u> for the winter which will easily see him finished. I am thinking of going at the [Greek] Anthology next. What do you say to it? (Burton to Smithers, 24 September 1890; HL)

Probably the most important period in Burton's professional life was the East Africa expedition of 1856-59, and Burton's correspondence does more to illuminate the Nile controversy than any of the Burton biographies. Burton's interest in the sources of the White Nile was evident in his letters as early as October 1853, when he wrote Norton Shaw from Cairo:

> I hear that the Geographical has been speaking about an expedition to Zanzibar. <u>Dhakilak</u> as the Arabs say—"I take refuge with you." I shall strain every nerve to command it or rather get the command—and if you will assist

me I'm a made man. I want Platte [unidentified] with me & a young fellow called Taylor [possibly Bayard Taylor, author of *Journey to Central Africa*] to do the actual instrument work & self. Only plenty of time! And a few muskets in order to carry things with a high hand. (RGS)

The following letters illustrate how Burton evolved his plan of discovery for the East Africa expedition. On earlier journeys to Arabia and Somalia, his linguistic skills had allowed him to gather information unknown to other travelers, and he now identified three goals for the expedition: (1) to locate and explore the "Sea of Ujiji" (Lake Tanganyika) and to document the ethnography and produce of the area, (2) to locate and explore the rumored northern "Ukewere Lake" (Lake Victoria), and (3) to locate and follow the rumored trade route across Africa east to west. The coordinates Burton quotes in his letter of 19 April for the rumored location of the sources of the Nile correspond exactly with the actual location of Lake Victoria. In November 1853, Burton wrote Shaw:

> Krapf just arrived from Zanzibar with discoveries about sources of White Nile, Kilimanjaro and Mts. of Moon which remind me of "de Lunatico"—I have not seen him but don't intend to miss the spectacle especially to pump what really has been done & what remains to be done. . . . About Zanzibar I have plenty of sound practical reasons why a mission there is highly advisable. A scientific mission of course. It is one of the headquarters of slavery—the Americans are quietly but surely carrying off the commerce of the country—and it has vast resources quite undeveloped. As a native I found out a spy of old Mohamet Ali who let me into all kinds of secrets about the country and wanted me to accompany him. I should have done so had I not been bound for Arabia. (RGS)

In December 1853, Burton wrote Shaw:

But Zanzibar appears to be the field. Krapf will meet you in England. He is, I hope, only my John the Baptist, I must be au courant of his discoveries. (RGS)

Burton's magnificent trip to Harar proved literally his first footsteps along the greater path to the lake regions of Central Africa. He said as much to Norton Shaw:

> My success at Harar has emboldened me & I have applied for a 2nd years leave. The Court of Directors will not, I think, refuse it, especially if it be at all backed up by the Roy. Geog. Soc. My plans (public) are to march southward to the Webbe Shebbelli and Ganana. Privately & "entre nous," I want to settle the question of Krapf and "eternal snows." There is little doubt of the White Nile being here abouts. And you will hear with pleasure that there is an open route through Africa, to the Atlantic. I heard of it at Harar & will give the whole account. (RGS)

The following letters illustrate Burton's systematic preparations for the expedition and his clear and detailed vision of its goals. In April 1856 Burton wrote Norton Shaw:

> I venture to request through you that the Roy. Geog. Soc. of Great Brit. will afford me their powerful aid in carrying out my original project of penetrating into Easter Africa. . . . I am prepared to start alone & if proofed [sic] necessary—disguised as an Arab merchant. Should, however, the R. Geog. Soc. induce toward an expedit, under the idea that a virgin country of such an extent as the line proposed could scarcely be investigated satisfactorily by a single traveller, I shall be happy to place before them a detailed scheme for preparations in the interior. (RGS)

On 19 April Burton wrote:

> The R.G.S., desire, I believe, to form an expedition pri-

marily for the 1) purpose of ascertaining the limits of the Ujiji Lake, 2) secondarily to determine the exportable produce of the interior & the ethnography of the tribes. . . . Proceeding to India, at the close of next Sept. I would there make preparations of the journey. An order from Govt. would enable me to collect from the vessels in Bo. [Bombay] Harbour a sufficient number (from 10-12) of the Swahili blacks [a marginal note, penciled in by Burton at a later date reads, "Not Swahilis—runaway slaves"] used in the steamers as cool trimmers & coal-hands. . . . I have already had the honour to record my willingness to proceed alone to E. Africa. Yet it would scarcely be wise to [chance all] upon a single life when 2 or 3 travellers would at all times be safer & in case of accident more likely to preserve the results of their labours. I should therefore propose as my companion, Lt. Speke of the B.A. if added with a sergeant or noncommissioned officer for the purpose of amistry & sundrys we should be enabled to perform a more perfect work.

The R.G.S. would doubtless not be contented with a mere exploration of the Ujiji Lakes. It is gen. [generally] believed [by Arab merchants] that the sources of the White R. [Nile] are to be found in the mass of mountains lying between 1 S & 1 N lat, & 32 & 36 S. Long. Moreover, the routes of Arab caravans who in 18 mths. have crossed Africa returning from Beneguela to Mozambique, force upon us the feasibility of exterior exploration. These two are separate & distinct objects. They would, however, be greatly facilitated by a preparatory exped. to the Un. Lakes as the information there procured by an intelligent eyewitness would serve for the better guidance of his successors. (RGS)

Had Burton succeeded with his plan, he would have become the greatest geographer of his day. His natural curiosity and thirst for adventure, combined with his scholar's skills, should have guaranteed him success. As it was, Burton's failure to gain full glory from the expedition was not the result of a lack of courage or planning but of more subtle flaws. Burton was no diplomat and, then as now, raising money for an expedition depended as much on public relations finesse as the ability to get the job done. Burton had been so critical of the British Navy, the Indian Army, and the Colonial Office in his books that his only supporters were a few friends in the R.G.S. No matter he had an excellent plan; Burton's support would only be grudging at best.

Burton was eventually given a thousand pounds by the government but this was not nearly enough to carry out even one section of the plan. Burton would have to cut back on his European staff, put up his own money and, even then, he would not have enough to pay his porters and guards their full salaries and tips. He had originally wanted three to four Europeans to join the expedition, and now he could barely afford one. His friend Dr. John Steinhauser was unavailable so he settled for Lt. John Speke, a critical mistake.

Lt. John Hanning Speke was a keen hunter who planned to use two of his three years of leave from the Indian Army hunting wildlife in Africa. He had a vague plan of searching for the source of the Nile as part of his hunting expedition but had no specific route and no linguistic skills which would help him proceed. Speke had been refused permission to travel on the African mainland because of danger from hostile tribes and was waiting at Aden when he met Burton's party bound for Somaliland. Burton agreed to help Speke out by making him a member of the expedition and assigning him the job of exploring the Wady Nogal.

Speke's participation in the Somali expedition was not a success. In fact, Speke's difficulties with his guide were directly responsible for the attack on Burton's camp at Berbera on 18 April 1855. During the attack Speke was gravely wounded and barely escaped with his life. Sometime during the attack, he ducked inside his tent to reload and Burton called out to him to stand his ground or the Somalis would think he was retreating. Speke took that as an insult to his courage and nursed his fury at Burton ever after.

Speke would have other causes for bitterness toward Burton as well. As commander (and financial sponsor) of the Somali expedition, Burton had considered Speke's collection of animal skins property of the expedition and sent them as research specimens back to India. Burton also considered notes kept by members of the party to be property of the expedition, and included Speke's notes in his official report and in his own book about the journey, *First Footsteps in East Africa*. Speke never voiced his objections to Burton directly about these matters, so Burton was unaware of the hostility he had aroused until later, in Africa, when it was too late.

Ironically, Burton went to great lengths to make sure Speke could accompany him to Africa. He even sailed with Speke to Bombay to plead for an extended leave for Speke from the Indian Army. Once Burton and Speke arrived in Zanzibar, Burton wrote George Balfour:

> People here tell frightful stories about danger and difficulty of the journey and I don't believe a word of it. Hamerton has been very ill but is recovering. Rebman [sic] is still at Mombas. We are in excellent health and spirits. So <u>adieu</u> and with Speke's compts.

Even as the two explorers were ready to set out from Zanzibar, Burton seems to have been completely unaware that the man he was trusting as a vital assistant and companion was actually a bitter rival waiting for his revenge. John Speke wrote his mother from Zanzibar about Burton:

> Wishing I could find something more amusing to communicate than such rot about a rotten person. . . . I have

now had ample analogous proof that B never <u>went</u> to Mecca or Harar in the common acceptance of the word but got artful natives to take him to those places, & I won't swear he did many a trick at their instigation. (QK)

This sensational letter from the Quentin Keynes collection is presented here for the first time. None of the modern Burton biographers has been aware of its existence, and it gives us a disturbing glimpse of John Speke's true feelings about Burton before the Nile expedition ever began.

In spite of desperate hardships, "Phase 1" of Burton's plan was successfully completed. The Ujiji Lake (Lake Tanganyika) was located and its eastern shoreline charted. Now "Phase 2" could be attempted. Burton wrote Norton Shaw from Central Africa on 24 June 1858:

We left the Lake of Ujiji about a month ago & are now halted at this main depot of Arab trade. Capt. Speke has volunteered when he & the rest of the party are sufficiently recovered from their present state of universal sickness, to visit the Ukewere Lake of which the Arabs give grand accounts. It lies nearly due North of Unyanyembi at a distance of from 12 to 15 marches. There we shall be enabled to bring home authentic details of the four great waters which drain Eastern & Central Africa viz the Nyassa, the Chama, the Ujiji Lake & the Ukewere. On Capt. Speke's return we shall lose no time in repairing to the coast which if we pass safely through Ugogo we may hope Dv. to reach about December of this year.

We have both suffered severely from sickness. We are compelled to travel from Unyanyembi to Ujiji during the wet monsoon & in the same season to embark in open canoes exposed to wind & rain, sun & dew and when on shore sleeping in mud, to explore the Lake—a labour of about a month. During this time we endured great hard-

Frontispiece from Burton's copy of *Journal of the Discovery of the Source of the Nile* (1863), by John Hanning Speke (Burton Library 1679).

ships and ran not a few risks.

Our limits on the Lake were laid down by the savagery of the Natives—as it was a man was unfortunately shot by my Portuguese servant during an attack.

Capt. Speke has suffered from the sequela of fever having lost his sight so as to be unable to read, write or observe for some time. The addition to which during his first voyage, some venomous insect crept into his ear, producing violent pain glandular swellings suppuration & finally deafness. Both I & my Portuguese servant have been subject to the distressing blindness. Besides this I have had a kind of numbness in the arms, hands & lower extremities & am still unable to walk or ride except in a hammock carried by Wanyamwezi porters. . . . Our asses, 30 in number all died, our porters ran away, our goods were left behind, our black escort became so unmanageable as to require dismissal, the weakness of our party invited attacks & our wretched Belochis departed us once in the jungle & throughout have occasioned an infinity of trouble.

We deeply regret that the arrangements for the expedition were not upon a more liberal scale, with £5000 we might, I believe, without difficulty have spanned Africa from East to West. . . . On the 20th Novr., 1857, Capt. Speke addressed to you a letter urging the necessity of arrangements for our guide & attendants. The late Lt. Col. Hamerton, H.B.M.'s Consul & N.E.I.C.'s Agent at Zanzibar advanced out of the public money no less a sum than $500 to our guide & promised him an ample reward & a gold watch in case he brought us home alive, an event then considered highly improbable. To the Jemadar of Belochis he gave $25 and to each soldier $20. These are sums which we could not afford nor can we on our return pay the high salaries promised in our presence to these men. By Said bin Salim, the guide, $1000 would be expected, by each Beloch—13 in number—$100, and by each slave,—in all 15—about $60. We have already expended at least £500 out of our private resources. . . . I venture to urge this subject most genially upon the Expeditionary Committee of the Royal Geographical Society, unless Lt. Col. Hamerton's promises be fulfilled by his successor, we shall be placed in a most disagreeable position at Zanzibar. (RGS)

In this letter we find Burton drawing the attention of the R.G.S. to the problem of underfunding and the need to pay his porters and guides salaries promised them by the late Lt. Col Hamerton. Burton was aware that he would not have nearly enough money when he returned to Zanzibar but what he could not have guessed was that his enemies (including Speke and Hamerton's successor, Consul Rigby) would see to it that he alone was blamed for the shortage.

Another important aspect of this letter is Burton's report that Speke had volunteered to investigate the northern lake as soon as he felt up to it. Burton himself could barely see and couldn't walk at all and, further, he needed time to write up his reports about the ethnography and exportable produce of the area, thus fulfilling one of the main goals of the expedition.

In the course of events, allowing Speke to go to the lake alone was the great mistake of Burton's career, and any man less the scholar and more the competitor never would have done it. But Burton felt secure in his position. He was, after all, the commander of the expedition. He had conceived it, financed part of it, identified its goals through his own research, and he knew that he alone possessed the intellectual capacity to give the expedition its substance. Speke was making this trip to the northern lake based on information only Burton could have gathered. We have seen how three years previously, Burton had reported the existence of the northern lake and even quoted exact coordinates from his Arab sources. Burton even knew how many marches they were away from the lake. So Speke was given the opportunity to exact revenge on Burton and capture the glory as "discoverer" of the Nile, all because of Burton's naivete, generosity, and dedication to the goals of the expedition. How tragic it was that after so much effort and sacrifice, he stood two weeks away from his goal and let glory slip away.

When Speke arrived at the lake he was nearly blind and all his instruments were lost or broken. He could not establish altitudes, or the latitude or longitude of the lake. His language skills were so poor he could only get minimal information from the locals. No wonder that when Speke returned to Burton claiming he had found the source of the Nile, Burton refused to support the claim to the R.G.S. until they had made a thorough investigation using proper instruments. But the expedition was out of supplies, living on credit, and the two explorers were in desperately poor health. Burton decided to lead the caravan back to Zanzibar. Totally unaware of Speke's animosity and Speke's plan to betray him, Burton gave him full credit for his work. In a letter to the R.G.S. he reported as follows:

RFB/Shaw   Khutu, Eastern Africa
                                          1st January, 1859
Sir,

I have the honour to acknowledge the receipt of your letter dated 2nd, Febr. 1857. I forward one copy of a Field Book & a Map by Capt. Speke, & take this earliest opportunity of transmitting his road map & field book to the Nyanza Lake (or Ukwere)—which he has been successful in discovering—his general map of our exploration similar to those formerly supplied but including our return route through Usagara & by another Southern line & his corrections of the Masai & Northern roads. These however, demand further enquiry & we particularly request that all documents now forwarded be not submitted to the public until they shall have received due revision at Zanzibar.

For the information of the Exped. Comm. I have the honour to report that in the total absense of all instructions and [in the want] of the supplies necessary to open up or to pursue our researches another path, our caravan has returned by the eastern road to Khutu (distant about 13 marches from the coast). Here it is halted for a time. Our refractory porters refuse to march upon any port but Kautu. We refuse to provision them for any other port then Kilwa which we would visit for the purpose of inspecting the lower course of the Ruaha or Rufiji River. The most obstinate will win the day, but I cannot, at the moment, exactly decide which party is in the predicament.

In conclusion, I have the honour to inform the Exped. Committee that on the 7th Dec., ult., I applied Officially to the Gov. in C. Bombay for 6 mths. additional leave (on behalf of my companion and myself) after the conclusion of the 2 yrs. granted by the Ct. of Dir. & that I hope the Society will lend me their powerful aid in obtaining an extension necessary to complete operations upon the base of exploration.

I have sir, etc., RFB

From Aden, Burton sent another report to the R.G.S. mentioning the northern lake. This letter has never been sufficiently analyzed by Burton's biographers, yet it is critical to an understanding of the Nile controversy.

Aden April 1859

A fresh attack of fever & general debility will delay me for a short time on the route to England where both Capt. Speke & I are about to proceed on medical certificate given by the Civil Surgeon of Aden. Capt. Speke will lay before you his maps & observations & two papers, one a diary of his passage of the Tanganyika Lake between Ujiji & Kasengi [sic] and the other his exloration of the Nyanza, Ukerewe or Northern Lake. To this I would respectfully direct the serious attention of the Committee as there are grave reasons for believing it to be the source of the principal feeder of the White Nile. The position has hitherto been placed by almost universal consent in the region Northwards of Mt. Kenia [sic]. But as the S.W. Monsoon & the S.E. Trades both exhaust their stores of humidity upon the Southern slopes of that great Equatorial line, the Lunar Mountains of ancient geography of which Kenia is, as far as can be ascertained, the Northern limit, we are entitled to believe that the Northern or leeward slopes of these mountains would not be so copiously watered as to send forth a surplus considerable enough to form the "White Nile." I have the honor to be, Sir, Your most obedt, servant,

        Richd. F. Burton, Commg.
        E. African Expedition

This letter, and the others previously quoted, establish that Burton had originally seen the northern lake as the probable source of the White Nile and that, had he not been prevented from doing so, he would have marched straight to the northern lake and made a thorough investigation of the primary source of the Nile.

Speke knew that Burton understood the significance of the northern lake. Speke also realized that Burton could, by rights, claim command of the next expedition to the northern lake—the expedition which would undoubtedly settle the question of the Nile. Speke knew, under those circumstances, that the best he could hope for would be the shared glory as second-in-command of the expedition. Given his competitive nature and the hatred he felt for Burton, this was an unacceptable alternative. Speke's only options in the matter were desperate ones, to claim credit for discovering the sources of the Nile, and to destroy Burton's credibility as commander of the expedition.

When Burton and Speke sailed together to Aden, Burton was already involved in compiling his notes from the expedition although his health was still severely impaired. Engrossed in his work and needing time to recover his health, he encouraged Speke to carry on to England without him. This was a second crucial error. As the two men said goodbye to each other, Speke said to Burton "Goodbye, old fellow. You may be quite sure I shall not go up to the Royal Geographic Society until you come to the fore and we appear together. Make your mind quite easy about that."

Speke arrived in London on 8 May 1859. On 9 May, he met with Sir Roderick Murchison and informed him of his discovery and theories and, on that first day, secured Murchison's support and assurance that he would be given command of the next expedition. When Burton arrived later in the month, he found Speke's name already linked with the new Nyanza Lake (Victoria) and a campaign under way to stir the fires of controversy against him. The break with Speke was now apparent to Burton, and in the following months the depth of Speke's bitterness became increasingly obvious.

When the two men appeared before the Expedition Sub-Committee of the R.G.S. on 20 June, it was arranged that in future explorations:

> considering the vastness of the field of inquiry and the respective special qualifications of Captains Burton and Speke, the preferable course would be, that they should proceed . . . by two distinct and independent routes.

The minutes of the subcommittee meeting of 20 June also record that Speke was encouraged to:

> at once commence arrangements for prosecuting the dis-

coveries which he has already made in the direction of Nyanza, and the supposed courses of the White Nile.

Burton had proposed to the committee that he disguise himself as an Arab merchant and travel via Berbera and Ganana along the caravan routes to the "reputed Snowy mountains from which the head-waters of the Nile are supposed to flow." The committee concluded that Speke's return should be financed and carried out as soon as possible and that Burton's plan would be considered when he had recovered his health and felt ready to undertake the venture.

Burton must have anticipated by then, as did the members of the committee, that his personal dispute with John Speke, the criticism that was still rife regarding his responsibility in the Berbera incident, and the hostility felt toward him by the government officials at Aden would hinder his travels through the territory he had proposed. Even if the R.G.S. was sincere in its interest in his plan, the obstacles that might be placed in his path by resentful government officials would plague him at every step. Burton's outspoken manner, his talent for controversy, and, finally, Speke's successful maneuvering combined to place him in an impossible position. There was enthusiasm and financial support for only one Nile hero, and Burton's acquiescence in the plan to proceed by "independent routes" was virtually an admission of defeat.

As Gordon Waterfield has pointed out in his introduction to the reprint of Burton's *First Footsteps in East Africa* (1966), the Nile controversy was "a serious set-back to Burton's career as an explorer" at a time when he most needed the financial and political rewards that success would have provided. With the reorganization of the India Office in 1858, which incorporated the East India Company, Burton's name was stricken from the latter's list of officers (because he had been serving outside their jurisdiction) and was not added to the new list. This brought Burton's career in the Indian Army to an end, at a time when his prospects as an explorer seemed to be ending as well.

Burton had prepared for the systematic exploration of the East African lakes not only in order to establish the true source of the White Nile but with the expectation that this discovery would be the crowning achievement of his career as an explorer. Isabel writes in her memoirs that when Burton proposed to her before going to Africa, he vowed that he would return to her and seek a position as consul to Damascus. The discovery of the source of the Nile would be the culmination of one career, and afterward he could pursue another that would allow him more time to devote to his wife and to his scholarship.

After Burton's death in October 1890, Isabel brought his body home to London for burial in St. Mary Magdalen Catholic Church, Mortlake, Surrey. Isabel built for Burton a mausoleum quite unlike any other in the world. It was a twelve-by-twelve-by-eighteen stone Bedouin tent, reminiscent of the ones she and Burton had used on their travels together in the wilds of Arabia. Both Isabel and Richard had written of their times camping among the tribesmen, and some of Burton's best writing described the sights and sounds of their romantic life there together. So it was with this memory in mind that Isabel laid Burton to rest in his last safari tent and decorated the interior of the tent with camp furnishings: a charcoal brazier, hanging lanterns, and a *narghilah,* or water pipe. When Isabel died in 1896, her casket was placed beside Burton's in the mausoleum.

In 1974 the Royal Geographic Society raised a sum of money to restore Burton's tomb. Vandals had broken parts from the outside of the mausoleum but it was not known whether they had damaged the contents of the tomb or if the Burton bodies had been disturbed in any way. In June of 1974, Quentin Keynes and I were invited by the Society to examine the interior of the tomb. As we entered the tent we could see that, in fact, no damage had been done. The caskets of Sir Richard and Lady Burton lay side by side in the gloom, with the contents of the tomb undisturbed. We were touched to see that Isabel had placed one of Sir Richard's favorite walking sticks across the

As we were leaving the tomb we commented on the long leather straps decorated with brass bells, which hung from the peaked roof of the tent. Burton had made many references in his writings to the Bedouin tradition of hanging camel harnesses across the roofs of the tents, and how he loved to listen to the tinkling of the camel bells as the desert wind blew them back and forth in the night. As I turned to leave the tomb, I noticed a small pile of rusted metal—copper, lead, and wire—at my feet. Examining the wall near them I found, fixed to it, the remains of what appeared to be a battery-operated armature that had long since rusted and fallen to pieces. Still attached to the wall were part of the armature and a bit of wire pointing toward the roof. I felt a lump in my throat and, I confess, a tear in my eye as I realized that Isabel had designed the armature so that she and her husband—as though on safari in the wilderness—could lie together once again, and for all time listen to the tinkling of the camel bells.

Burton as Autobiographer

by John Hayman

Burton is not alone among Victorian writers in not having written an autobiography. Victorian writers seem usually to have felt it indecorous to draw attention to themselves in deeply probing self-scrutinies. It was considered appropriate for an individual of some eminence to leave a record of his public career, but memoirs of this kind (by such writers as Darwin or Huxley) lack the intimate and introspective qualities we expect of an autobiography. Some individuals managed to maintain social decorum while writing probingly of their personal lives by addressing their autobiographies to their children and denying any interest in publication: Leslie Stephen's *Mausoleum Book* is such a record. Some even disguised their autobiographies by writing of themselves in the third person and pretending that the work was written by another; Thomas Hardy provides perhaps the most elaborate instance of this strategy.

Many Victorian writers felt that the Romantic writers of the turn of the century had improperly exposed their souls to the world at large—and they were intent on distinguishing themselves in one way or another from such writers. Macaulay is perhaps the most formidable critic of this exhibitionism. He remarks on "those modern beggars for fame who extort a pittance from the compassion of the inexperienced by exposing the nakedness and sores of their minds" (*Edinburgh Review*, August 1825).

Burton may be associated with the declared unwillingness to write of oneself which is so prevalent among Victorians, and he was also critical of others who wrote intimately of themselves. Speke was one such individual. In his book *What Led to the Discovery of the Source of the Nile* (1864), Speke confessed at one point to having experienced a "nervous sensibility I never knew before," and Burton noted marginally in his copy of the book: "Silly egotist" (Burton Library 1680, p. 188).

Burton apologized on several occasions for any appearance of egotism in his own writings. At the opening of a lecture, for example, he remarked: "it is necessary to dispose of a few preliminaries which must savour of the personal. I hope you will not say of the egotistical" (*Sir Richard Burton's Travels in Arabia and Africa: Four Lectures from a Huntington Library Manuscript,* 1990, p. 15). He seems even to have felt some distaste for personal recollection, perhaps because he found himself often recalling earlier disappointments and grievances. In *Sind Revisited,* which describes his return to the region where he had first been stationed abroad, he remarked, "how very unpleasant to meet one's Self, one's 'Dead Self' thirty years younger" (1877, p. 257). On another occasion he declared, "I cannot imagine anything more trying than for a man to meet himself as he was" (Isabel Burton, *The Life of . . . Burton,* 1893, 1:1).

According to Isabel Burton, it was a gentlemanly modesty which disinclined Burton to write about himself. "It was," she remarked, "one of his asceticisms, an act of humility, which the world passed by, and probably only thought one of his eccentricities." He might be outrageous in the personal disclosures (and subterfuges) of a conversation, but "in print," she continued, "he never could be got to talk about himself" (*Life of Burton,* 1:vii). But Isabel's testimony occurs, rather ironically, at a point in her biography where she is introducing the autobiographical writings which Burton dictated to her. Despite all his protestations, Burton is in fact to be associated not only with those who declared a reluctance to write about themselves but

Photograph of Isabel Burton by J. B. Rottmayer, Trieste, ca. 1888 (Burton-Smithers correspondence, Huntington Library).

also with those (often one and the same) who overcame their reluctance.

First, then, I should like to consider the writings of Burton which are undeniably autobiographical. Of these, the earliest is the so-called "Little Autobiography," which first appeared as a postscript to *Falconry in the Valley of Indus* (1852) and was subsequently included in Isabel's *Life of Burton* (1:151-58; quotations are from this section of *Life*). In this sketch, Burton presented his credentials for writing about India, in response to a review in which he had been described as a "young man" with "some very extreme opinions." In his "Little Autobiography," Burton turned the tables by declaring that "the Eastern mind . . . is always in extremes" and by insisting on his familiarity with all manner of people in the region, "low as well as high." In this context Burton did feel it legitimate to write of himself, in a militant act of self-defense. As a reviewer remarked, *Falconry in the Valley of Indus* contained "a Narrative, an Autobiography, and a Protest" (quoted in N. Penzer, *Selected Papers on Anthropology, Travel, and Exporation*, 1924, p. 14).

In the autobiographical section, however, Burton does not simply present his credentials for writing about India. He begins: "After some years of careful training for the Church in the north and south of France, Florence, Naples, and the University of Pisa. . . ." This is an extraordinarily misleading way to present the wayward and restless traveling of the Burton family, and quite at odds with Burton's other accounts of his early years. Elsewhere he emphasizes how the unsettled life of his family left him unprepared for higher education and the professions.

In writing of these early years and of his subsequent period at Oxford in the "Little Autobiography," Burton displays both the inclination to write of himself and his sense that it was appropriate to hold such an inclination in check. He negotiates this rather awkward position by adopting a tone which moves between the facetious and the severe. Of his time at Oxford, for example, he remarks:

> To be brief, my "college career" was highly unsatisfactory. I began a "reading man," worked regularly twelve hours a day, failed in everything—chiefly I flattered myself, because Latin hexameters and Greek iambics had not entered into the list of my studies—threw up the classics, and returned to old habits of fencing, boxing, and singlestick, . . . and sketching facetiously, though not wisely, the reverend features and figures of certain half-reformed monks, calling themselves "fellows."

The detachment from the self that is arranged by this facetious tone is arranged in another way when Burton writes of having disguised himself in Sindh as "a half-Arab, half-Iranian, such as may be met with in thousands along the northern shore of the Persian Gulf." At such a point, Burton refers to himself in the third person, as "Mirza Abdullah of Bushire, . . . a vendor of fine linen, calicoes, and muslims":

> Thus he could walk into most men's houses, quite without ceremony; even if the master dreamed of kicking him out, the mistress was sure to oppose such measure with might and main. He secured numberless invitations, was proposed to by several papas, and won, or had to think he won, a few hearts; for he came as a rich man and he stayed with dignity, and he departed exacting all the honours.

When he was traveling, then, the disguise permitted Burton some fine liberties—and in writing of the experience in his "Little Autobiography," he was able to write of himself with detachment and decorum.

Almost a quarter century was to pass before Burton formally turned again to autobiography. Then, on a voyage to India in 1876, at the age of fifty-five, he composed an account of his life up to his mid-thirties—"he dictating and I writing," according to his wife (*Life of Burton*, 1:vii). The journey to India, where he had been stationed almost thirty-five years earlier, was itself a looking backward, a review of his life, and it clearly encouraged autobiographical recollection. A decade later, in 1887, he permitted Francis Hitchman, who was preparing a biography of Burton, to use these autobiographical chapters. According to Isabel Burton, Hitchman had appealed to Burton for assistance, with some reference to his "poverty, sickness, and large family" (Isabel Burton to Leonard Smithers, 16 February 1888, Burton-Smithers correspondence, Huntington Library), and Burton had with characteristic generosity sent him the manuscript. From considerations of respect, or perhaps out of sheer laziness, Hitchman merely altered the personal pronoun from *I* to *he*, and presented the composition as his own. Subsequently, Isabel Burton presented the same material—but in its original form—as the opening seven chapters of her *Life of Burton*.

Burton had apparently intended to write further chapters of his autobiography. On 12 March 1888, Isabel Burton wrote to Leonard Smithers from Trieste: "We begin tomorrow his autobiography seriously & I shall be glad if you will make that simple fact as public as possible." Perhaps she hoped to turn her husband's attention from the erotica he was working on at the time, but in this she seems to have been unsuccessful. A year and a half later, in a letter to Smithers also written from Trieste, Burton himself remarked: "As regards my autobiog. it must wait till the present load is off my brain" (12 September [1889]). Finally it was decided that the autobiography should be postponed until 1891, when Burton was to retire from the consular service, and consequently his death prevented the completion of the project.

Interested as she was in her husband's giving an account of his life, Isabel Burton must surely have had some misgivings about the undertaking, for she was by no means at ease with the passages he had dictated to her on the voyage to India. In another letter to Smithers, she indicates this:

> I begged to be allowed to erase many little things in the early biography, which he dictated to me, & his only answer & always was, 'I will not have it altered. If a biography is written, it must be a true photograph with its good & its evil & I like my boyish faults to be put in as well as my good qualities.' (18 February 1888)

As a result, when she included the autobiographical sections in her biography, Isabel Burton had to be content with some footnotes in which she either dissented from her husband's account or pressed it into a more flattering mold. He was not, she insists, physically "plain," as he described himself, but "the handsomest and most attractive man [she had] ever seen" (1:3n). He had found it necessary to disappoint his father and cut short his time at Oxford because, she insists, "he could not obey his father, and also carry out the destiny for which he was best fitted and obliged to follow" (1:90n). One may wonder whether Burton delighted in shocking his wife by dictating experiences which he knew she would find upsetting—even whether the enterprise was a deliberate test of her obedience.

Certainly there is much in the dictated autobiography that must have dismayed Isabel Burton. In particular, there are indications of a quite extraordinary violence, which make it seem that Burton is intent on showing the origin of his nickname "Ruffian Dick." His hostility to those authority figures of his youth—his early governesses and tutors—is perhaps especially remarkable, and he seems sometimes to have had his brother and sister as allies. There is, for example, his account of their treatment of a governess who vigorously preened herself when complimented on her sense of responsibility: "A jerk of the arm on her part brought on a general attack from the brood; the poor bonne measured her length upon the ground, and we jumped upon her" (1:22). Later, a teacher of the violin fared no better: "Our professor was a thing like Paganini, length without breadth, nerves without flesh, hung on wires, all hair and no brain, except for fiddling.... In a fury of rage, I broke my violin upon my master's head" (1:38). Later still, Burton remarks, when "we were getting too old to be manageable," another tutor "very nearly received a good thrashing" (1:45). It is perhaps understandable that Burton's mother was happy to hand over her brood to hired help, but it seems she also became involved in their violent ways. There is the celebrated story of her once inviting Burton, his brother, and his sister to admire the apple-puffs in a pastry shop and then pass on, having learned a lesson in self-restraint. "Upon this," Burton writes, "we three devilets turned flashing eyes and burning cheeks upon our moralizing mother, broke the windows with our fists, clawed out the tray of apple-puffs, and bolted."

Burton's aggressive temperament is not only directly apparent from such recollections. It is also reflected in random details in his narrative—for example, his account of the animals he recalls having kept. There is the bull terrier: "its box-headed and pink face . . . scratched all over during a succession of dog-fights and various tussles with rats, a creature so thoroughly game, that he would sally out alone in the mornings, and kill a jackall single-handed" (1:96).

Burton's language also reveals this same aggressive energy in more unexpected contexts. There is, for example, the imagery of attack in the descriptions of his forays into the different languages of India. He writes of "wearying of Greek and Latin" at Oxford and attacking Arabic; of later giving "some twelve hours a day to a desperate tussle with Hindustani"; of "attacking with renewed vigour" the Guyrat language; and of "throwing aside" Sindi for Maharatee (1:77, 107-8, 122). Of his progress, he writes at one point: "The neck of the language was now broken" (1:81). In introducing this concern with languages, Burton remarks that "sensible men who went out to India took one of two lines—they either shot, or they studied languages" (1:110). Burton was not at all interested in shooting. "There is," he said, "an eternal sameness in the operation of shooting, which must make it,—one would suppose, very uninteresting to any but those endowed with an undue development of Destruction" (*Falconry in the Valley of the Indus*, p. vii). It would seem, however, that Burton brought to the study of languages some of the fierceness of one bent on destruction.

So far, I have been remarking on Burton's explicitly autobiographical writings. But it is of course possible to think of his travel books as massive chapters in a continuing autobiography, and it is to his writings on travel that I now wish to turn. Burton himself indicated their distinctly autobiographical emphasis in the title of his most celebrated travel account, *Personal Narrative of a Pilgrimage to El-Medinah and Meccah* (1855). Isabel Burton accepted such guidance and included lengthy passages from the travel books in her *Life of Burton*.

We may, however, distinguish in the travel narratives between the direct, even intimate, glimpses of himself that Burton permits at times and the oblique autobiography which they seem also to contain. This oblique autobiography sometimes takes the form of his apparently writing of himself while nominally writing of another. In his first travel book, *Goa, and the Blue Mountains; or, Six Months of Sick Leave* (1851), he writes, for example, of an unnamed lieutenant who planned an elopement with a nun. It has generally been assumed that the incident relates closely to circumstances in Burton's life, and it may therefore be significant that the incident is narrated by the unnamed lieutenant's servant, Salvador, which seems calculated to distance the events even further from Burton. All the same, Salvador's account of the lieutenant makes him appear uncannily like a slightly idealized portrait of Burton himself:

> He could talk to each man of a multitude in his own language, and all of them would appear equally surprised by, and delighted with him. Besides, his faith . . . was every man's faith. He chaunted the Koran, and the cir-

> cumcised dogs considered him a kind of saint. The Hindoos also respected him, because he always ate his beef in secret, and had a devil (i.e., some heathen image) in an inner room. At Cochin he went to the Jewish place of worship, and read a large book, just like a priest. Ah! he was a clever Sahib that. (pp. 73-74)

The lieutenant and Burton clearly share a skill in languages and an ability to take on the life of their surroundings by means of disguise. The parallel is even more apparent when Salvador says of the lieutenant: "he was not a man to be daunted by difficulties; in fact, he became only the more ardent in the pursuit" (p. 77).

In his next travel book, *Scinde; or, The Unhappy Valley* (1851), Burton's disguise is more elaborate and artful. For in this book he creates an extravagant persona which seems in fact to permit him to express some aspects of his personality. The persona is that of a vigorous (even bullying) guide who conducts Mr. Bull (or the British reader) on a tour. To an unusual degree, the procedure involves double bluff. For within a few pages, the guide is addressing Mr. Bull as "My dear, fat, old, testy, but very unblood thirsty *papa de famille*" (p. 4). This persona of the forthright guide may develop from Burton's uncertain relationship with his British reader, but it also becomes a pointed means by which Burton may express a characteristically brusque attitude. His contempt for the cant of the bourgeoisie (as represented by Mr. Bull) and his contempt for the cant of conventional travel books are vividly expressed through this guise.

> Now, a year or two after you return home you will probably forget *les actualités* of the scene. You will find it necessary to suppose facts, as you will have discovered that the Childe Harold style 'goes down' society's throats much more glibly than that of Mattheus or Smollett. . . . Therefore you will become impressionable, romantic, poetical, semi-sublime, *et cetera*.

And one of these days, sir, when I detect you describing to a delighted lady audience, 'the strong—the overpowering emotion with which you contemplated the scene of Alexander's glories'; when I hear you solemnly asseverating that 'never before did the worship of water or water-gods appear to you so excusable, as in observing the blessings everywhere diffused by this mighty and beneficient stream'—

Then sir, I shall whisper in your ear, 'No, Mr. Bull, you did nothing of the kind.' (pp. 185-86)

Clearly, Burton's impatience with cant and his forthrightness found deft expression in this work.

But Burton does not reveal his disposition only by such indirect means in his travel books. As I have remarked, he also permits the reader some direct and intimate glimpses of himself. In *Scinde; or, The Unhappy Valley*, for example, he refers to one section as "a quiet little bit of egotism" (p. 89), and he writes with scarcely concealed feeling of the sense of neglect that an individual may experience when serving abroad:

Men are separated from family and friends, and made to feel that separation too. Letters, which during the first year of expatriation arrived regularly each mail, gradually diminish in number, shrink in size, cease altogether. They know that when they return home their relations will think and find them *de trop*—the average heart cannot stand up against ten years thorough separation—that their friends will have ceased to care for them, that their acquaintances will have clean forgotten them. (pp. 92-93)

A personal animus is evident enough here beneath the show of objectivity and detachment.

This distinctly personal note is also to be heard in *Scinde; or, The Unhappy Valley* when Burton writes of experimenting with hashish:

> I have often taken the drug, rather for curiosity to discover what its attraction might be, than for aught of pleasurable I ever experienced. . . . The first result is a contraction of nerves of the throat, which is anything but agreeable. Presently the brain becomes affected; you feel an extraordinary lightness of head as it were; your sight settles upon one object, obstinately refusing to abandon it; your other senses become unusually acute—uncomfortably sensible. (p. 262)

The passage is scarcely "confessional." In fact, Burton again moves toward generalization about the experience. But the account is openly based on personal experience. Hashish is described in an altogether different way in Burton's more academic book on the region, appropriately titled *Sindh, and the Races that Inhabit the Valley of the Indus; with Notices of the Topography and History of the Province* (1851). Here Burton merely remarks that hashish "is believed to cause fearfulness, and great vivacity of imagination; it produces unnatural hunger, followed by painful indigestion" (pp. 169-70). There is no acknowledgment of personal experience. The two very different passages on hashish focus for us Burton's characteristic movement between the explicitly subjective and the apparently objective.

In writing both a "personal narrative" and an anthropological analysis concerned with the same region, Burton began a practice which he was to adopt at other times. Following his African exploration of 1857-59, for example, he presented his strictly geographical findings in the *Journal of the Geographical Society*. In his two-volume publication, *The Lake Regions of Central Africa* (1860), he presented a more personal account. Of the book-length publication, he remarked in the preface: "I have not attempted to avoid intruding matters of a private and personal nature upon the reader" (p. viii). Instead, he had attempted to adopt a range of concern and tone. "I have drawn two portraits of the same object," he remarked, "and mingled the gay with the graver details of travel, so as to produce an antipathetic cento" (p. vii). This movement between the subjective and the objective, the informal and the formal, the amusing and the instructive, the popular and the learned, is altogether characteristic of Burton—and it is also the means by which he could express different aspects of his personality.

Again, Burton himself is a helpful guide to our recognizing these different aspects of his being, since on occasion he explicitly remarks on his dual sense of himself. And it is this sense of duality—and its embodiment in his writing—which I wish now to consider.

His book *The Lake Regions of Central Africa* is especially revealing. Some thirty pages into the account, he begs the reader's indulgence for his personal emphasis:

> Excuse, amiable reader, this lengthy and egotistical preface to a volume of adventure. . . . As we are to be companions—not to say friends—for an hour or two, I must put you in possession of certain facts, trivial in themselves, and all unworthy of record, yet so far valuable, that they may enable us to understand each other. (p. 27)

Subsequently, Burton writes in detail of his "impaired health" and "depression of spirits," of being "weak and depressed, with aching head, burning eyes, and throbbing extremities" (p. 71). And then, in one of those extraordinary flashes of self-revelation, he remarks quite explicitily on his divided sense of his personality. "I had," he remarks, "during [a] fever-fit, and often for hours afterwards, a queer conviction of divided identity, never ceasing to be two persons that generally thwarted and opposed each other" (p. 84). This experience of duality was not limited to this single occasion, nor was it connected only with a fevered condition. In her *Life of Burton,* Isabel reports an oculist's discovery late in Burton's life that his right eye required no. 50 convex and his left eye no. 14 convex. She writes that upon being informed of this, "He turned to me and said, 'I always told you that I was a dual man, and I believe that that particular mania when I am delirious is perfectly correct'" (2:268). At another point in her *Life of Burton*, Isabel provides an interpretation of this sense of duality, which she apparently considers flattering to herself and to their marriage. In a footnote, she remarks: "Richard used always to say that, psychologically speaking, he was convinced that he was a spoiled twin, and that I was the broken or missing fragment" (2:164n). Clearly, she concurred with Robert Browning's notion that a man had two fronts: one to face the world with and one to show a woman when he loved her. She declared that in society "he was like the 'Man with the Iron Mask'"—apparently relaxed and open—but in fact "beautifuly reserved" and intent on revealing of himself only what he chose to reveal. With a rather touching naivete, she took it upon herself in her biography "to lift the veil as to the *inner* man" (1:ix).

Her sense of an outer and an inner man was, however, anticipated by Burton's own "queer conviction of divided identity." Moreover, his writings attest to this division. They show him to have been a champion of established order who was nonetheless repeatedly in conflict with authority, as well as an intensely patriotic Englishman who was at the same time highly critical of virtually all aspects of church and state. They also offer more intimate glimpses of his divided temperament—for example, of the vacillation between indolence and activity, between passivity and assertiveness. His Aunt Georgina's first memory of him, he said, was of his lying on his back, "in a broiling sun, and exclaiming, 'How I love a bright burning sun!'" (*Life of Burton*, 1:19). He later saw this delight in the sun as prophetic of his pleasure in the tropics. And in *Zanzibar; City, Island, and Coast* (1872), he was to give expression to the relaxing sensuality of the setting:

> Truly prepossessing was our first view of the then mysterious island of Zanzibar, set off by the dome of distant

hills, like solidified air, that form the swelling line of the Zanzibar coast. Earth, sea, and sky, all seemed wrapped in a soft and sensuous repose, in the tranquil life of the Lotus Eaters, in the swoon-like slumber of the Seven Sleepers, in the dreams of the Castle of Indolence. (1:27-28)

"All," as he remarks (with even clearer sexual implication), "was voluptuous with gentle swellings." Characteristically, however, Burton does not simply celebrate such sensual appeal. The intensely active part of his personality urged him to be up and doing—learning languages, prospecting for gold, inquiring into sexual customs. After a while, he therefore finds Zanzibar to be "over-indolent." Again, in strikingly sexual (and sexist) terms, Burton writes:

Without a single element of sublimity, soft and smiling, its sensuous and sequestered scenery has no power to spur the thought, to breed an idea within the brain. The oppressive luxuriance of its growth combined with the excess of damp heat, and possibly the abnormal proportion of ozone, are the most unfavourable conditions for the masculine. (1:146)

Finally, in this account of Zanzibar, Burton declares: "We learn at last to loathe thee." The conflict between indolence and exertion could scarcely be indicated more frankly, and it seems clearly to have developed from Burton's "divided identity."

On other occasions, this conflict might lead simply to a restless alternation between indolence and activity, the settled and the roaming. Near the opening of *Personal Narrative of a Pilgrimage to El-Medinah and Meccah,* he wrote of "the thoroughbred wanderer's idiosyncracy [sic]":

After a long and toilsome march, weary of the way, he drops into the nearest place of rest to become the most domestic of men. For a while he smokes the 'pipe of permanence' with an infinite zest; he delights in various siestas during the day, relishing withal deep sleep during the dark hours; he enjoys dining at a fixed dinner hour, and he wonders at the demoralisation of the mind which cannot find means of excitement in chit-chat or small talk, in a novel or a newspaper. But soon the passive fit has passed away; again a paroxysm of ennui coming on by slow degrees, Viator loses appetite, he walks about his room all night, he yawns at conversation, and a book acts upon him as a narcotic. The man wants to wander, and he must do so, or he shall die. (memorial ed., 1893, 1:16)

Again, the use of generalized statement does not conceal the underlying animus of the passage.

Burton did not claim to have brought about for himself that reconciliation of opposite or discordant qualities which Coleridge described as the supreme imaginative achievement. He associated his "queer conviction of divided identity" with conflict and thwarting. But he found balance, reconciliation, and wholeness in the life of a literary figure he revered, the figure of Camoens. Burton's study and translation *Camoens: His Life and His Lusiads* (1881) has long been recognized as containing a good deal of self-portraiture. Again, then, it would seem an instance in which Burton wrote of himself in the guise of another. Like Burton, Camoens had served in the army in India; he had traveled in Arabia; he had fallen into disfavor in his native land as a result of his writings; and he had been hard-pressed for money during a life of virtual exile. Of special interest to us here, however, is Burton's comment on Camoens's sensibility —since by Burton's account, it was characterized by both forthrightness and delicacy, assertiveness and sensitivity, a reconciliation of duality (once again expressed in terms of gender): "We find in Camoens," Burton notes, "none of the weakly, sickly Humanitarianism of our modern day" (1:56). And yet he was, Burton declares, distinguished by "his woman-like sensitiveness and sensibility— that curious touch of the feminine temperament in a doughty man-at-arms and an undaunted traveller" (1:59-60).

One further aspect of his sense of a "divided identity" may serve to bring these remarks together. It concerns the persistence of the theme of nostalgia, or "homesickness," in Burton's writings.

At first glance, it may seem surprising that Burton should have expressed nostalgic feelings. Such a sentiment may seem at odds with the dominant image of Burton as the explorer always pressing forward rather than looking back; indeed we have seen evidence of his extreme reluctance to look into the past. But as I have been suggesting, such a view takes account of only a part of Burton's identity, that curiously divided identity which was susceptible to extremes of opposed feeling.

Indeed, Burton may have experienced nostalgia so poignantly precisely because it came upon him unexpectedly—in the course of a swing from an opposite extreme. In describing his departure for Africa in 1857, for example, it is the elation of departure and the excitement of new experience which he initially gives expression to:

> One of the gladdest moments, methinks, in human life, is the departing upon a distant journey into unknown lands. Shaking off with one effort the fetters of Habit—the leaden weight of Routine—the cloak of carking Care, and the slavery of Home—man feels once more happy.

Later, when he introduced this passage, from an article in *Blackwoods* (vol. 83, Feb. 1858, p. 200), into his book-length account, he remarked of it: "Somewhat boisterous, but true" (*Zanzibar*, 1:17). Certainly its tone contrasts strikingly with the nostalgia and melancholy that frequently color his accounts of Africa. "The absence of all association," he writes, "the sense of loneliness and estrangement, the absurd distance from friend and family seem to diffuse an ugliness over every African river, however fair." Similarly, in *Abeokuta and the Camaroons Moun-*

tains (1863), he remarks on "the constituents of beauty in [the] landscape" and of his failure to respond to this beauty:

> The scene before me wants neither grandeur nor beauty; there is a gorgeous growth around; hill, water, forest, and homestead—the constituents of beauty in landscape—all are present; yet, brooding over them all, darkening sun and sky, and clothing earth with sombre hues, is the sadness of a stranger-land. (1:65)

Burton had no such feeling of nostalgia in Arabia since he had a mystical feeling that a visit to Arabia was a homecoming—a return to his place of origin. In the foreword to *The Book of the Thousand Nights and a Night* (1885), he remarked: "The land of my predilection, Arabia, [was] a region so familiar to my mind that even at first sight, it seemed a reminiscence of some bygone metapsychic life in the distant Past" (1:vii). In Africa, amid profuse vegetation and varied terrain, he felt the lack of human association. In Arabia, amid the "rare simplicity" of the desert, his life was enriched by a sense of his earlier life in the region.

This engagement with the life of Arabia was also accentuated by Burton's taking on a disguise in his travels there. The adoption of a persona must have accentuated Burton's sense of being a "divided personality," but it also gave coherent form to this feeling of division. An invented self also assumed and replaced a "real self," and perhaps Burton found pleasure in disguise for this reason. The divided aspects of his being no longer thwarted each other. They were ordered within the device of a disguise.

But Burton's disguise was the device of a traveler; it did not provide him with a settled role in a stable society. Burton's nostalgia is finally the more poignant because he had no secure sense of home—and no sure sense of identity either. It seems fitting that Burton's place of birth should have been a matter of dispute among his biographers. Even after his marriage, it cannot be said that he settled anywhere for long; his wife was frequently faced with the injunction to "pay, pack, and follow." A late portrait by Albert Letchford of Burton "at home" in his study is curiously impersonal. Burton is seated at a table and viewed from behind, a lonely figure in a rather bare room. In looking at the portrait, one has no sense of contact with the subject, and Burton does not appear at ease in the setting. Letchford also painted a more celebrated portrait of Burton as a formidable fencer, but the portraits seem of different individuals—or, of course, of an individual with a "divided identity." In the painting of Burton in his study, the room could be anywhere, the figure virtually anyone.

In his autobiographical reminiscences, Burton himself reflected on the effect of homelessness when describing the constant movement of his family when he was young:

> It is a *real* advantage to belong to some parish. It is a great thing, when you have won a battle, or explored Central Africa, to be welcomed home by some little corner of the Great World, which takes a pride in your exploits, because they reflect honour upon itself. In the contrary condition you are a waif, a stray; you are a blaze of light, without a focus. (*Life of Burton*, 1:32)

In his autobiographical writings Burton aimed to bring much into focus, perhaps above all a clearer sense of his divided self.

Photograph of Burton by G. L. Formosa, Malta, ca. 1889 (Edwards H. Metcalf Collection, Huntington Library).

Burton's Review of Doughty's *Arabia Deserta*

by Stephen Tabachnick

On 28 July 1888, Richard F. Burton's review of Charles M. Doughty's *Travels in Arabia Deserta* was published in the *Academy*. Twentieth-century partisans of Doughty have never forgiven Burton for this review. Anne Treneer, for instance, claims that in this case Burton wrote in a "manner discreditable to himself" (*Charles M. Doughty: A Study of His Prose and Verse*, 1935, p. 27). David G. Hogarth, Doughty's biographer, writes that Burton could not conceal his "jealousy of a feat surpassing his own" Arabian explorations (*The Life of Charles M. Doughty*, 1928, p. 129). R. H. Kiernan, following Hogarth, also accuses Burton of jealousy but then adds in extenuation that "Burton was ill, a disappointed man, and near the end of his days" when he wrote the review (*The Unveiling of Arabia: The Story of Arabian Travel and Discovery*, 1937, p. 276). This paper will attempt to show that these judgments are wrong and that Burton's review is highly intelligent, balanced, and valuable. Moreover, the review tells us as much about Burton's character as about Doughty's.

I would like to thank J. H. Prynne, Librarian of Gonville and Caius College, Cambridge, for permission to quote from the Burton letters in the college's Doughty collection.

Doughty's thousand-page book appeared during the first week of January 1888 through Cambridge University's Pitt Press, after having been rejected by several commercial publishers. In a unique—some would say quirky—style composed of varying amounts of Chaucerian English, authentic Arabic utterance, and Doughty's own special brand of correct English, it tells of the haps that befell Doughty in central Arabia from November 1876 to August 1878 as a professed Christian Englishman devoid of passport, money, and respect for Islam. This basic plot, filled with head-on religious disputes and overwhelming hardships, is interwoven with lengthy and disordered disquisitions on Arabian geography, geology, and anthropology.

The book's famous first sentence reveals a rich, bilingual style and mentality:

> A new voice hailed me of an old friend when, first returned from the Peninsula, I paced again in that long street of Damascus which is called Straight; and suddenly taking me wondering by the hand "Tell me (said he), since thou art here again in the peace and assurance of Ullah, and whilst we walk, as in the former years, toward the new blossoming orchards, full of the sweet spring as the garden of God, what moved thee, or how couldst thou take such journeys into the fanatic Arabia?"

Any reader would immediately find himself in a strange relationship with this unusual book. We will soon see how the expert, demystifying, and very direct Richard F. Burton reacted to it. A look at the two men's unpublished correspondence preceding the review will set the scene.

The letters from Doughty to Burton in the Huntington Library and their counterparts from Burton to Doughty in the Caius College Library, Cambridge, show that the two explorers began well—Doughty as the aspirant to Burton's good opinion and help in securing a publisher and Burton generous with his advice and good wishes. But when the correspondence began, around 1884, Doughty had not yet read Burton, and Burton had not read Doughty except perhaps for his strictly archaeological and geographical publications.

The first letter we have, from Doughty to Burton dated 21 October 1884, indicates that it was preceded by earlier correspondence. Doughty speaks of his difficulty in finding a publisher for *Arabia Deserta,* and he consults Burton about an area around Medina. He says that he has told his mapmaker, with regard to the wadi, or dry river-bed, between Tebuk and Medina, to "follow only Captain Burton." He criticizes the Royal Geographical Society map that accompanied his own 1884 lecture.

Burton, no doubt pleased with Doughty's compliments, replies in a postcard from Trieste dated 28 October 1884 that Chatto and Windus might be a potential publisher. Burton then calls attention to some lava fields, omitted in Doughty's work, that Burton had mentioned in his *Personal Narrative of a Pilgrimage to El-Medinah and Meccah.* Finally he states modestly that "all my knowledge of the subject" of the fields, until Doughty's advent, came from the Germans Wetzstein and Ritter. He mentions his possible return to London in early spring.

On 13 November 1884 Doughty writes that he still has not found a publisher, but thanks Burton for the information about the lava fields. He criticizes George Augustus Wallin's geography and Wetzstein's use of the Arabs' reports about the fields. He expresses the hope of seeing Burton in London in the spring. He mentions that he has recently been in Italy, but apparently he did not attempt to see Burton in Trieste.

Then on 27 January 1885 Doughty writes cheerfully to Burton that William Wright and Robertson Smith, perhaps the premier British contributors to Semitic studies in the nineteenth century, have suggested that he submit his book to the Pitt Press. He adds that he has been reading "with great interest and great pleasure your Pilgrimage and further I am quite happy to find that there is nothing in my writing which disaccords" with

Burton's view of the Arabs. He goes on to say the same about Robertson Smith's "Letters from Jidda and Taif" and compares his own observations with those of "you learned men," Burton and Smith. He admits that he has not read Burton's *Midian*—a reference to Burton's two books about his two northern Arabian explorations for gold in 1877 and 1878, when unbeknownst to them both they were not far away from one another, during Doughty's own Arabian wanderings. Finally, he asks Burton to send Smith a letter recommending *Arabia Deserta* for publication. And again he comments on the unreliability of Wetzstein's informants.

Burton responds in a letter with no place and no date indicated, probably written in February 1885 in Trieste. He asks to be remembered to Robertson Smith, whose company he has always enjoyed. He agrees that Wetzstein is a good artist but a less good geographer. He also mentions that he is now translating the sixth volume of the *Arabian Nights* and has "the bad taste to say that I greatly enjoy the work"; and that he is still set on coming to London in April or May. In terms of his later review, the most important part of his letter is as follows: "Very glad that you find the Pilgrimage agree with your observations; and now please read the three volumes of Midian."

We do not know what was said, if and when the men met in London in the spring of 1885, or when they had dinner together there in 1886, but their good relations continued, for in the last letter in this series, written on 6 January 1888 to Burton, Doughty states that the two volumes of *Arabia Deserta* will be published that very week, and hopes that review copies "may be almost immediately in your hands for the *Academy,* as the editor wishes me to send them on." He goes on to say, indicating a lost communication, "I think you ask 'What I would have particularly noticed in them?' [but] I prefer to have them, without note or comment, in your distinguished and generous hands."

So having suitably flattered Burton, Doughty entrusted his book to him for review, confident that Burton's opinion would be completely favorable; and Burton, having read such a letter and knowing Doughty's earlier praise of his own work, surely believed that his *Pilgrimage* and Midian books would play a role in Doughty's treatment of related subjects. These expectations were a clear prescription for disaster, as an examination of the review will now show.

Let us begin by saying that Burton, unlike many reviewers, actually read and understood *Arabia Deserta:* his many detailed annotations, usually if not always concerning factual matters of topography and terminology, in his copy of *Arabia Deserta* (Burton Library 1954) prove that. In the review's five and a half closely printed columns, he discusses in detail the book's composition, literary quality, contribution to previous knowledge, and linguistic information, as well as its position on the question of whether or not a traveler in Arabia should confess Islam to make his passage easier.

Because he intended it to be his contribution to the English language as well as to Near Eastern studies, *Arabia Deserta* took Doughty six years to write and another four to revise and publish. Burton addresses the issue of timing immediately. Although he finds that "the geographer, the epigraphist, and the student of Arabic will attach the highest importance" to Doughty's work, these experts will also "admire the while at the author's worldly unwisdom." In Burton's view, Doughty had inexplicably delayed writing and publishing his book, "systematically frittering away the interest of his subject" in infrequent articles and allowing other explorers "in the meanwhile to visit the lines he had opened and to devance him before the reading world." As a professional explorer, Burton was understandably protective of his own achievements and was correspondingly eager to lay claim to them in writing; his own bulky *Pilgrimage* appeared only three years after his journey of 1853 and his Midian books followed his explorations there even more quickly. His vast bibliography far exceeds Doughty's in quantity. As a man spread over many fields and projects, Burton simply could not understand someone slower and more deliberate.

This leads us to the second point, the literary quality of travel accounts as Burton sees them. Even if Burton was not one to linger over fine style when reportage of discoveries was at stake, he is clearly sensitive to literary quality, calling Doughty's tale "right well told" despite its "affectations and eccentricities, its prejudices and misjudgements." He praises in particular Doughty's characterization of individuals, as well as his topographic descriptions. But quoting *Arabia Deserta*'s first sentence, which has also stopped many subsequent readers in their tracks, Burton asks "Whether Mr. Doughty is justified in adopting, for a prosaic *recit de voyage*, a style so archaic, so involved, and at times so enigmatical, however fitted it may be for works of fiction, and however pleasant for the reminiscences of days when English was not vulgarised and Americanised." While Burton was ready to tolerate, even to applaud, stylistic flights in poetry and fiction, he clearly felt that a travel book (like his own *Pilgrimage*) should be a straightforward, "prosaic" denotative account, a scientific report-cum-adventure narrative rather than a work of high art. The truth about one's travels and observations, according to Burton, should be expressed clearly and directly, not approached obliquely through artistic prose and involved philosophical meditations. Here Burton's position as a scientific demystifier and literary realist opposed to Doughty's mystification and proto-magical realism becomes clear. And Burton's straightforward pronouncement that Doughty's "punctuation runs daft" is certainly the truth. But since Burton was a master-linguist and poet, his failure to understand, as we now do, that Doughty's style alone of all English prose styles succeeds in capturing authentic Arabic rhythms is a surprising disappointment, perhaps the one genuine failure of insight in his review.

After admitting that he cannot comment on all matters of importance in such a huge book, Burton announces that he will consider "what mainly interests me—the discovery of Medain

Salih and the Arabism of the glossary"—in other words, Doughty's contributions to previous archaeological, geographical, and linguistic knowledge. But first, in a brief aside, Burton states that he agrees with Doughty about the uselessness of the Foreign Office and its consuls—surely an interesting and revealing observation, since Burton was himself a consul when he wrote this review. And then, from this unexpected, if minor, point of agreement with Doughty, he moves to a major complaint against him: "Mr. Doughty informed me that he has not read what I have written about Arabia; and this I regret more for his sake than my own. My 'Pilgrimage' would have saved him many an inaccuracy [while] . . . My three volumes on Midianland . . . would have supplied a standard of comparison other than Petra." Is Burton's claim true or false—an egotistical display of pique or a justified criticism?

As we have seen in his letter of 27 January 1885, Doughty claimed to be reading Burton's *Pilgrimage* while he was revising *Arabia Deserta*, but no reference to Burton whatsoever appears there. So Doughty was either insincere in his praise of Burton's book or simply decided not to cite it, for unstated reasons. And apparently Doughty never bothered to read Burton's Midian volumes at all (despite Burton's clear request in his letter circa February 1885 that Doughty do so), although they cover some of the same areas that Doughty visited. Burton's annoyance is justified. Although his *Pilgrimage* does not discuss much geography that was not already known, there is no doubt that a reading of his important books about the Midian area would have been beneficial for Doughty: on his Midian expeditions, Burton did after all survey many Nabataean cities of the type Doughty describes, did collect ores for very precise scientific assessment in London as Doughty could not, did make many important geographical discoveries, and did provide an extremely good map, as D. G. Hogarth himself acknowledges in his comprehensive study, *The Penetration of Arabia* (1904).

After justifiably taking issue with Doughty's neglect of his own work, Burton questions Doughty's statement that before his trip no one had described the lava beds of northern Arabia. While it is true that Doughty made major contributions to the descriptions of two large fields, it is also true that Burton, in his *Pilgrimage* and Midian books, notes lava fields, and that many others had discussed such lava fields in contiguous areas of Syria and Palestine. Surely Doughty should at least have mentioned—if he was even aware of—some of these sources. Instead of mentioning and then criticizing Wetzstein, for instance, as he does in his letters, Doughty simply ignores him in *Arabia Deserta*. Perhaps unsurprisingly, in a recent assessment of Doughty's geology Reginald Shagam and Carol Faul conclude that he willfully neglected the previous and far superior work of Otto Fraas and Louis Lartet, among others (Tabachnick, ed., *Explorations in Doughty's "Arabia Deserta,"* 1987, pp. 163-85).

Burton himself is never guilty of the fault of willfully neglecting his predecessors. As has often been noticed, even in his description of the *kaabah* (the enclosure of the holy stone at Mecca) in an appendix to his *Pilgrimage*, he shines the spotlight on J. L. Burckhardt, not himself. Simply put, Burton had the scientific mentality that is always ready to enter into dialogue with peers; Doughty, although nominally a geologist, did not. How galling it must have been for Burton to find a man in some ways less capable but more arrogant actually making more important discoveries, perhaps for the second time in Burton's life (the first would have been his experience with Speke). But whatever his personal feelings, Burton fully acknowledges the importance of Doughty's discoveries, attacking only his arrogant claim to total sovereignty over knowledge.

Burton then discusses Doughty's treatment of language, one of his own strong points and one of Doughty's weak ones: Burton after all knew somewhere between twenty-five and sixty languages (depending on the biographer, and on our definition of what a language as opposed to a dialect is), and Arabic, both spoken and literary, was among his favorites. Doughty learned only spoken Arabic, with difficulty, and knew some Italian and perhaps French at the time he wrote *Arabia Deserta*.

Burton finds that the glossary of Doughty's book, revised by Professor M. J. de Goeje, has unusual value. In Burton's view, although Doughty lacked "the fine ear" of Burckhardt, he was able to capture many peculiarities of speech, particularly the previously unstudied Nejdi Beduin accent, giving "Ullah" for "Allah," for instance, albeit without realizing that he was reporting only a dialect rather than a more standard Arabic. However, Burton may go too far in claiming that no Arab ever said "Ullah Akbar" for "Allahu Akbar" [God is great]; isn't it possible that Doughty heard a quickly uttered, shortened version in a spoken dialect, much as we might hear someone say "all best" for "all the best"? But we must conclude that despite occasional linguistic puritanism like this, Burton mixes praise and blame judiciously in this area, as in most others in this review.

Perhaps the most important—because most revealing—area of disagreement Burton saves for last: the matter of disguise, which quickly becomes a debate about personal integrity. Doughty made it clear that he could not respect those Europeans who traveled in disguise and feigned Islamic belief. As he puts it in a still-notorious statement in *Arabia Deserta*, quoted by Burton: "It had cost me little or naught to confess Konfucho or Socrates to be apostles of Ullah; but I could not find it in my life to confess the barbaric prophet of Mecca and enter under the yoke into their solemn fools' paradise" (*Arabia Deserta*, 1979, vol. 1, p. 253). The undisguised and religiously absolute Doughty paid the price for his willingness to confront Islam and the Arabs' customs directly at every turn. He was attacked by mobs, treated with suspicion by the authorities, not allowed admittance into Mecca, and he had to suffer the blows and taunts of an anti-Christian sheikh all the way from the outskirts of Mecca to Taif. We might term this the anthropology of confrontation, and we can learn much about nineteenth-century

Arabian and British attitudes from it, as the anthropologist Robert Fernea has recently pointed out (Tabachnick, ed., *Explorations in Doughty's "Arabia Deserta,"* pp. 201-19). Or as one of Doughty's contemporaries explained it, writing (anonymously) in the scientific journal *Nature* (28 June 1888, p. 195), Doughty quite simply harbored an old-fashioned prejudice against Islam that ill-equipped him for study of the Arabs. For Doughty himself, his confrontational journey quickly became a living death; and we begin to suspect that his oft-touted integrity was perhaps a self-inflicted and unnecessary religious test of some kind.

In contrast, the disguised, relativistic Burton got along famously with the inhabitants of Egypt and Arabia alike: he was a great drinking companion for an Albanian soldier and a superb fighting companion aboard his pilgrim ship. Most of all, however, he was able to see the pilgrimage and the cities of Medina and Mecca as they were in 1853 and record every detail for all time. His is anthropology from the inside; he tells us what the pilgrims do and say among themselves, and he became one himself to some degree, even while feeling fear and pride rather than the pilgrim's religious ecstasy.

To Burton, as he stated in his review, Doughty's persecutions were "wholly brought on by the traveller's imprudence and perverseness," and we are not surprised when he concludes that Doughty's book really teaches "the need of a certain pliancy in opinions, religious and political," in a traveler. For Burton, conscience is a "geographical and chronological accident," and indifference to others' customs and sensitivities, whatever one thinks of them, is inexcusable. Here, in my view, we have the essential Burton—the man able to flirt with many religions before deciding on "self-cultivation, with due respect for the rights of others" (*Kasidah*) as a life-creed, the man far more flexible in his appreciation of other cultures than were the vast majority of his contemporaries. Certainly Burton had his obvious personal prejudices—particularly, distorted views of Jews, contempt for blacks, and a belief in phrenology—all suitably garbed in pseudo-scholarly apparatus. But he had perhaps fewer prejudices than most other Victorians, including not only Doughty but the Indian Muslim Begum of Bhopal, who made the pilgrimage shortly after Burton did and was far more critical of the Arabs than he ever was. (An enlightening analysis of South Asian Muslim attitudes toward the pilgrimage is Barbara Metcalf's essay, "The Pilgrimage Remembered," in Dale Eickelman and James Piscatori, eds., *Muslim Travellers,* 1990. See also Nawab Sikander Begum of Bhopal, *A Pilgrimage to Mecca,* trans. Mrs. Willoughby-Osborne, 1870.)

In the end, do we learn more about the Arabs from Burton's disguised, sympathetic view from the inside, or from Doughty's undisguised, confrontational view from the outside? Perhaps we need both perspectives to begin to understand another culture fully. But Burton cannot be accused of a lack of integrity for choosing one method of investigation over another, or for having the ability to pass as an Arab, which Doughty probably could not have done, even had he wanted to.

Given the fact that Burton was more adaptable and more ready to accept other cultures on their own terms than were Doughty and other Victorians, his final comment shows surprising chauvinism: "Mr. Doughty assures us that his truth and honesty were universally acknowledged by his wild hosts; yet I cannot, for the life of me, see how the honoured name of England can gain aught by the travel of an Englishman who at all times and in all places is compelled to stand the buffet from knaves that smell of sweat." Some have seen in such comments a clear sign of Burton's unqualified imperialism and his desire to use his knowledge of the East only to control it. But given what we know of his personality and experiences in England, in my view Burton is playing to the English gallery here—consciously or unconsciously trying to gain the respect of a British establishment whose culture he liked less than that of the East, and which always, with some reason, regarded him as an alien.

But in his disparaging comment that Doughty must go

"armed, not with the manly sword and dagger, but with a penknife and a secret revolver," we have the sword-loving Burton who felt that he, like his vision of the British Empire, could gain respect only by overt shows of force. It does not seem to occur to him that the Christian pacifist Doughty, by refusing to disguise himself, displayed a moral and physical courage that was comparable to Burton's own physical courage with a sword. But pacifism was not Burton's philosophy.

In his belief that he had to compel—rather than quietly earn—respect, whether from his own countrymen or from foreigners, Burton reveals a mental no less than a physical pugnacity that stood him well in the many controversies in which he was engaged. This pugnacity appears in his lively responses to critics of his *Arabian Nights*, for instance, in the correspondence columns of the *Academy* for 1888.

According to Jean Burton, a contemporary public controversy between Burton and Doughty and other scholars preceded Burton's review (*Sir Richard Burton's Wife*, 1941, pp. 331-32), but I have not been able to find any trace of it before or after the review, either in the *Academy*, or in James A. Casada's annotated bibliography (*Sir Richard F. Burton: A Biobibliographical Study*, 1990), or in any other biographical source pertaining to either Burton or Doughty. That such a controversy occurred would seem highly unlikely, since Doughty left for the Near East in February 1888 after writing Burton the friendly and optimistic letter of 6 January that I have quoted, and did not even return to Europe until a year later. Perhaps Jean Burton refers to lost letters that were written between Doughty's last of 6 January and the appearance of Burton's review. In any case, her remarks remain mysterious.

Whether such a controversy ever took place (either in written or oral form) in the Victorian period, one thing appears certain today, despite the claims of Burton's detractors: apart from some of its stylistic judgments and time-bound political opinions, Burton's estimate of *Arabia Deserta* appears entirely balanced and reasonable. All told, Burton wrote a very perceptive review of a great but difficult book.

Engraving of "The Prophet's Block" in Salt Lake City, made for *The City of Saints* (1861) and based on a drawing by Burton.

"The Captain Has Seen Utah without Goggles": The Mormons and Richard Burton

by M. Guy Bishop

Richard F. Burton visited Great Salt Lake City, the center of Mormonism, during the late summer and early fall of 1860. Burton biographers, however, have paid only passing attention to this adventure in the American West. There are several possible reasons for this. Most Burton scholars likely find his western trip much less exhilarating than the hunt for the source of the Nile or the risky undercover journey to the sacred Moslem cities of Mecca and Medina. Most of his biographers, excepting Fawn M. Brodie, likely have had limited exposure to Mormon history and thus have paid little attention to this episode in the man's life, viewing it more as a restful interlude than a serious scholarly investigation on Burton's part. In the words of Byron Farwell, it was "Sick Leave in Salt Lake City" (*Burton,* 1963). Farwell offered only a brief treatment, and observed, "Burton's purpose was to add Great Salt Lake City to the list of other holy cities he had seen." Fawn M. Brodie, who, because of her earlier biography of the Mormon prophet Joseph Smith, *No Man Knows My History* (1945), might have been expected to produce an enlightening look at the Captain's time in the city of the Saints, offered but a simple, superficial treatment; and Edward Rice, a recent biographer, says perhaps even less than most other Burton scholars about the visit to Utah. Burton bibliographer James A. Casada, who acknowledges that Brodie's *The Devil Drives* is "the best biography we have of Burton," also says nothing in his overview about the Captain's stay in Salt Lake City. Notes made by the biographers suggest no effort to understand this period of Richard Burton's life, beyond a quick look at Salt Lake City's *Deseret News* and Burton's own *City of the Saints*. Despite the many Burton biographies, we still have limited insight, beyond that given in his own narrative, into the Salt Lake City experience. Entirely missing from all of the studies is information concerning what the Saints thought of Richard Burton.

It is clear that Burton consulted the available contemporary literature on the Mormons. He noted in *The City of the Saints* that he had read the works of Jules Remy, John C. Fremont, and Howard Stansbury, but it is not known which of these studies he read before and which after the trip to Salt Lake City. The Burton Library, housed at the Huntington Library, contains an annotated copy of J. W. Gunnison's *The Mormons, or, Latter-day Saints, in the Valley of the Great Salt Lake* (Burton Library 1725). Fremont, Stansbury, and Gunnison were serving with the U.S. Corps of Topographical Engineers surveying the Great Basin when they met the Mormons. Stansbury's official report, along with Gunnison's more informal observations, served to inform interested parties about the Mormons.

Who were these American religionists Richard Burton sought to study in 1860? The movement founded by Joseph Smith, Jr., in upstate New York in 1830 was one of the most dynamic, and hated, of American sects by the mid-nineteenth century. To believers it was a restoration of the gospel of Christ. For opponents Mormonism was a fraudulent product of Smith's imaginative mind. And late twentieth-century scholars have interpreted the movement by turns as a product of antebellum American culture, a new religious tradition, or a rejection of the American pluralism of the 1830s and 1840s. Mormonism itself professed to be the sole repository of divinely sanctioned religious authority. Such was certainly a bold assertion—and one bound eventually to attract the attention of Richard Burton.

Before finally settling in the isolated Great Basin, the Mormons tried to build their vision of Zion in Ohio, Missouri, and Illinois. Yet each time, internal unrest or external persecution forced the followers of Joseph Smith to uproot and look elsewhere for a place to serve their God. In June 1844 Smith was lynched by an anti-Mormon mob at Carthage, Illinois. Within two years most Mormons packed up and moved west under the leadership of Brigham Young, the senior member of the church's Quorum of Twelve Apostles. Seeking a place which no one else would want, Young located the Saints in the Valley of the Great Salt Lake in the summer of 1847.

Contrary to their expectations, the Latter-day Saints' move relieved their sense of persecution for only a brief time. Their enemies were now at a greater geographical distance, but the verbal and written assaults continued. And the Mormons actually fueled the fire through some of their actions. Rumors that the Saints were practicing polygamy contributed to the anti-Mormonism in Illinois during the early 1840s. For a time they felt safe in the isolation of the Great Salt Lake Valley. Then the Mormon hierarchy, led by church president Brigham Young, publicly acknowledged their practice of plural marriage. Plurality, they believed, was a law of God. For nearly four decades polygamy was embraced by the Latter-day Saints. At the same time the Mormons attempted to perpetuate civil as well as religious rule by the church authorities. Gentiles, or non-Mormons, living in the Utah Territory regularly reported the Saints to be un-American, rebellious, and in dire need of federal control.

The middle and late 1850s proved a tragic time in Mormon-Utah history. Conflict with federal authorities in the Utah Territory heightened Mormon suspicions and fears. In response to ugly rumors of sedition spread by gentile residents and visitors, President James Buchanan ordered federal troops to Utah in 1857. While no bloodshed resulted directly from this act, in southern Utah a group of paranoid and misled Mormon frontiersmen joined forces with local Indians to massacre a party of gentile emigrants at Mountain Meadows. Although this action was taken without the stated approval of the church leadership, the national image of Mormonism was further tarnished.

When Richard Burton stepped down from the westbound stage at Salt Lake City on 25 August 1860, he entered a perplexing world. Burton was simultaneously honored as a notable visitor and distrusted as an outsider. The *Deseret News*, official voice of the Mormon community, heralded Burton's arrival by acknowledging, "The captain is a traveler of distinction, generally known as the Hajee [sic] Burton, pilgrim to Mecca, explorer of Hurrur [Harar], and discoverer of the great central African Lakes." Still, the Saints must have been apprehensive about how the famed explorer would judge them.

Contemporary scholars rarely saw the Mormons with anything but a jaundiced eye. Englishman Robert Baird, in a study of American religions published in 1845, wrote of the Latter-day Saints, "The annals of modern times furnish few more remarkable examples of cunning in the leaders and delusion in their dupes, than is presented by what is called Mormonism." Frenchman Jules Remy and Englishman Julius Brenchley, visiting Utah a few years before Burton, found polygamy "a barbarous and bestial thing" and marriage, among the Mormons, to be "destitute of all that gives it a character of delicacy and purity among Christians." It would have been a small wonder if some Mormons did not expect Burton to be equally critical.

Captain Burton stayed in Salt Lake City for just over one month and was, in his words, treated with "great respect" wherever he went. He talked with Mormons and gentiles, attended their worship services, wandered through the city stopping at stores and reading the local newspaper. In short, Burton made every effort to come to an understanding of Mormon culture.

On 31 August Burton had an audience with Brigham Young. The Mormon prophet was a man with a national, if not international, reputation. He had hosted several noted visitors to Salt Lake City. Remy and Brenchley, touring Utah in 1855, reported the Mormon leader to be a man of "superior intellect, [with] remarkable talent and profound ability in combining the heterogeneous elements of which his people are made up." New York City newspaper editor Horace Greeley met Brigham Young in 1859. Greeley found the Mormon leader to be a modest, pleasant man.

Of his initial impression upon being introduced to Young, Burton wrote, "He has been called hypocrite, swindler, forger, murderer—no one looks it less." When Brigham Young inquired as to why Burton had come, the English visitor responded that having read and heard much about Utah as it was said to be, "I was anxious to see Utah as it is." Whether this reassured the Mormon leader or not is unknown.

Burton noted the attendance of Mormons Daniel H. Wells, George A. Smith, Wilford Woodruff, and Albert Carrington at the meeting. According to Woodruff, Lorenzo Snow and Franklin D. Richards were also present. Wells was a counselor to President Young in the church's First Presidency; Smith, Woodruff, Snow, and Richards were apostles; and Carrington was Brigham Young's private secretary. Most of these men were part of Young's "inner circle" of advisers in the 1850s and 1860s. The meeting was deemed a pleasant one by the Mormons. "He [Burton] stayed about one hour," wrote Woodruff, and "conversation turned upon Capt. Burton's travels in India, Arabia & Africa." Norman Penzer observed in a letter to a fellow scholar, written in 1938, that Brigham Young received his British visitor cordially "since Burton had expressed himself in favor of polygamy." Although lacking any formal documentation, Penzer's observation may well be right.

George A. Smith served as church historian from 1854 until 1870 and was most helpful to Burton when he was writing *The*

City of the Saints. Apostle-historian Smith may have been officially assigned to assist Burton, but other less well-placed Saints also had much contact with him while he was in Utah. Mr. and Mrs. T. B. H. Stenhouse, for example, frequently accompanied Captain Burton. Burton stated that he saw T. B. H. Stenhouse "almost every day" while in Salt Lake City. The Mormon couple were a natural contact for Burton. Natives of the British Isles, they had both embraced Mormonism and migrated to the United States by 1855. Stenhouse, having proved himself as a Mormon missionary in England and Italy during the late 1840s and early 1850s, became an influential Utah journalist. A stalwart defender of the faith at the time, Elder Stenhouse "could never see any[thing] but the perfection of his system." His wife, Fanny, seemed to balance the picture for Burton. She "showed a highly cultivated mind," he observed, and was probably a major source in his examination of Mormon polygamy. The Stenhouses eventually were numbered among Mormondom's most notorious apostates: she for her exposés on polygamy and he for his support of the Bodbeite movement, a heresy which sought to transform Mormonism economically and socially during the early 1870s.

Another Mormon frequently seen with Captain Burton while he studied the religion and the community was Amos Milton Musser. Musser would also have been naturally drawn to Burton, since he had served a church mission in India. Burton was often accompanied by either Stenhouse or Musser on his frequent visits to the Church Historian's Office in Salt Lake City. They were a kind of intellectual entourage while he visited in the Utah Territory.

Apostle Wilford Woodruff also spent time with Burton. One day Woodruff escorted the Englishman on a tour of Brigham Young's house as well as gardens and shops. Afterward Burton went to the Church Historian's Office, where George A. Smith gave him an outline of the recent Mormon war with the United States. Smith also provided a history of affairs in Utah for the preceding five years. While both Woodruff and Smith were gracious men, it is equally certain that these Mormon leaders hoped to influence Burton's view of the Saints. And they just might have succeeded, as Richard Burton was sometimes accused of being an apologist for the Mormons. The *Christian Observer*, to cite one such example, using a veiled reference to Burton's penetration of Mecca, said, "Mr. Burton writes with the air of an apologist; sometimes we could believe him to be a Mormonite disguised."

Records from the Historian's Office journal make it quite clear that Richard Burton, whether apologist or objective observer, made every effort to understand the Mormons:

> 3 September 1860—Captain Burton called at 1:20 p.m. accompanied by A. M. Musser and T. B. H. Stenhouse. Talked about his travels and took notes of the principal circumstances connected with Mormonism the past four years. Staid about one hour.
>
> 11 September 1860—Captain R. F. Burton and T. B. H. Stenhouse called about 5 p.m. The Captain asked various questions about the country and its productions. Staid about half an hour.
>
> 13 September 1860—Captain R. F. Burton called in the p.m. and staid nearly an hour.
>
> 18 September 1860—Captain Burton came in the office and staid half an hour.

Although revealing little regarding what the Mormons may have thought of Burton, these journal notations do demonstrate a willingness to cooperate with him, and they certainly show no ill feelings.

Unfortunately, there are no extant diaries kept by either of the Stenhouses, and the journals of Amos Milton Musser make no mention of Burton. But a few sporadic references to him do appear in contemporary Mormon writings. In a letter written 7 September 1860 Wilford Woodruff noted that

> Captain Burton of the British Army, a notable traveler[,] has been visiting with us for some ten days.... He appears much pleased with his visit to and with President Young and friends and of the city in general.... He is much of a gentlemen, and he has traveled enough to throw off that prejudice which many feel towards those not of their political and religious faith.

On 3 October 1860 the *Deseret News* announced the departure of Richard Burton from Great Salt Lake City. Since the newspaper was the official voice of Mormondom at the time, the appraisal published there would seem representative of the view of the church hierarchy.

> As far as we have heard, Captain Burton has been one of the few gentlemen who have passed through Utah without leaving behind him—a disagreeable souvenir. The captain has seen Utah without goggles....

The next thing for Richard Burton to do, having completed the trip, was to write his book about the Mormons. Once again, Latter-day Saints in official and quasi-official capacities were most helpful to Burton. In June 1861 William C. Staines, a Latter-day Saint missionary in London, wrote to Brigham Young:

> Captain Burton is writing about us and he has requested me to forward him Books &c which I have done. [H]e was been appointed Counsel to [Fernando Po] which he has accepted. [H]e tells me he will correspond with you while he is in that country.

Whether Burton communicated with Brigham Young at that time is unknown. The two men did, however, correspond in

1873. Then, Young wrote a response to a letter from Richard Burton. He told Burton he was warmly remembered in Utah and proffered an invitation for a return visit. Young's letter was brief but friendly.

Since *The City of the Saints* and Jules Remy's *A Journey to the Great Salt Lake* were published in the same year, reviews comparing the two books were soon forthcoming. The *Edinburgh Review* noted, "It was an appropriate design on the part of the English Hadjee to visit the Mormon city." Like most gentile observations of the Mormons the *Review* article was focused predominantly upon polygamy. Referring to Remy's and Brenchley's resounding condemnations of the Mormon practice on moral grounds, the writer noted that Burton, by contrast, "makes no attempt to conceal his satisfaction at coming into contact with the fragments of much familiar Eastern life in the midst of what to him is the 'abomination of civilization.'"

The *London Review,* in another comparative analysis of the two books, found Captain Burton's study "in some respects the more reliable." Following a rather lengthy treatment, the article closed by summarizing each author's thoughts on Mormon children. Remy and Brenchley declared that children in Mormondom were "generally godless, licentious, and immodest," a condition they largely attributed to polygamy. Burton, on the other hand, found in Mormon youth "less premature depravity than in the children of European cities generally." Of course, it must be remembered that Richard Burton was never one to let the chance to slight Western or European society slip by him. This may also be further evidence that the Mormons' friendly and forthcoming reception of their well-known and influential visitor had proven successful.

Among the Mormons themselves Burton's objectivity was praised, even over a hundred years after *The City of the Saints* was first published. A review of Fawn M. Brodie's 1963 edition of the work evoked the following from Salt Lake City's *Deseret News:*

In the case of "The City of the Saints" his performance did not rank with his very best—notably his amazing "Personal Narrative of a Pilgrimage to El Medinah and Mecca"—yet it remains one of the most satisfying books about Mormonism. . . . When everyone else was writing with venom and jocularity about the Church of Jesus Christ of Latter-Day Saints, the open-minded Burton [wrote] fairly and comprehensively.

In the Mormon community and, in fact, throughout Europe and the United States, *The City of the Saints* and Richard Burton were, and generally continue to be, remembered as a look at Mormonism and polygamy. Perhaps it was only fitting that the man who penetrated the Moslem holy city and wrote about Eastern sexual practices should also find his reputation tied to the Latter-day Saints of Utah. Richard Burton would likely have appreciated the irony that his Mormon acquaintance Wilford Woodruff, then acting as president of the Mormon church, issued a manifesto ending the church's sanction of plural marriage on 26 September 1890—less than a month before Burton died at Trieste.

Additions to Burton's Bibliography

by Burke E. Casari

About twenty-five years ago, I began purchasing books by and about African explorers. I had no experience with book collecting and no knowledge of antiquarian book dealers, but by reading book reviews and biographies I began to get an idea of the works published in English by the major explorers and where I might find them. One of the first book dealers specializing in African materials that I became acquainted with was Phil McBlain, then living in Des Moines, Iowa, who welcomed me to his home and showed me his book collection. With his encouragement, I began to make lists of books I wanted, and I continued to add and delete titles as I made purchases. Over the years, I acquired books by Krapf, Barth, Bruce, Park, Burckhardt, von Hohnel, Salt, Casati, Junker, Nachtigal, Baker, Grant, Speke, and Burton—just a sampling of the authors that came my way.

I expanded my interests to include nineteenth-century magazines, journals, and newspapers. After some years of collecting, I made the decision to seek mainly the works of Sir Richard Burton. This meant I would include items not only on African exploration but on the Near East, translations, and such exotic works as *The Book of the Thousand Nights and a Night.*

Because of the cost and scarcity of some of Burton's titles, I obtained photocopies of a few of them. The New York Public

Library sent me a microfilm of *A Complete System of Bayonet Exercise*. Through Mr. Janes of the Sutro Branch of the California State Library, San Francisco, I obtained a microfilm of *Stone Talk*, the 1940 Works Projects Administration reprint. Much other material has been made available through the University of Nebraska Love Library interlibrary loan office, including Victorian periodicals, Ph.D. dissertations, and recent articles in publications not available at local libraries. Admittedly, a photocopy is not as exciting as an original edition. My interests, though, are not only in collecting itself but also in the contents of the works. I wanted to obtain access to as wide a variety of Burton's works as my time and income allowed, in order to understand the context of his diverse interests and activities.

For my own pleasure, I set about reading the footnotes to Burton's sixteen-volume translation of *The Book of the Thousand Nights and a Night*. This acquainted me with the variety and breadth of his interests and views on matters anthropological, sexual, and cultural, and led me to write for myself what would be called, as near as I can determine, an "olio"—an essay composed of or reliant on a melange, miscellany, or varia of material. This type of arrangement seemed to me to represent, by analogy, Burton's lifelong habit of keeping voluminous journals, notebooks, and diaries, and of adding marginalia in his own library materials. I included various chapters, with introductory statements, on Burton's footnoting, his use of dissimulation, and the experimentation in an early work that could become a pattern for a later one. In this exercise, I sampled the profusion of thoughts that often burst forth in Burton's footnotes. At one point in Burton's *Camoens: His Life and His Lusiads*, he says of Edward Quillian, a previous translator of this work, that his notes are nothing, "mere tags" (1880, vol. 1, p. 67). Burton observes in his *Os Lusiads*, in an entry entitled "Note": "believing in the 'liberty of footnotes,' I have appended a few." By the time Burton got around to his translation of *The Arabian Nights* a few years later, he demonstrated that a

A

COMPLETE SYSTEM

OF

BAYONET EXERCISE.

BY

RICHARD F. BURTON,

Lieutenant Bombay Army,

Author of " Sindh, and the Races that inhabit the Valley of the Indus;" " Goa and
the Blue Mountains;" " Falconry in the Valley of the Indus;"
" Scinde, or the Unhappy Valley;" &c. &c.

LONDON:
PRINTED AND PUBLISHED BY
WILLIAM CLOWES AND SONS,
14, CHARING CROSS.

1853.

Title page of Burton's own copy of *The Complete System of Bayonet Exercise* (1853), now one of the rarest of his publications (Burton Library 5).

footnote, or more properly a monograph, could turn the text into a mere tag.

Another project I began was a search for unrecorded articles, letters, and reviews by Burton as well as notices and ephemera about him. I spent weekends, over several years, looking through *Punch* magazine from 1850 to 1890, and turned up half a dozen ephemeral items about Richard and Isabel. It seemed clear from my review of *Punch* that many readers closely followed the activities of the Burtons and that they were associated in the public mind with adventure and unusual accomplishment. Next I reviewed sixty-five years of *Notes and Queries*, an easier task because unlike *Punch*, it has been well indexed for generations. From *Punch* and *Notes and Queries*, I graduated to *Fraser's Magazine* and *Blackwood's Edinburgh Magazine*. These periodicals contain reviews, articles, letters, and poems, but I found little by Burton that had not already been attributed to him. One exception was a group of letters published in *Fraser's Magazine*, in volumes 72 through 74, with the title "From London to Rio de Janeiro. Letters To A Friend" (1865-66); Penzer's *Annotated Bibliography of Sir Richard Burton* (1923) cites letters 1 through 4 only; Kirkpatrick's *Catalogue of Sir Richard Burton's Library* (1978) adds letters 5 and 6. It was not until James Casada's *Sir Richard F. Burton: A Biobibliographical Study* (1990) appeared that letters 7 and 8 were cited. My intent here is only to point out that it is not uncommon for a beginning researcher to accept the work of another without checking it. It is particularly easy to overlook items in some nineteenth-century periodicals because of the lack of an adequate index. The table of contents is often brief and may categorize items by subject, or by some arbitrary scheme devised by the editor—for example, sections like "Our Library," "Literature," and "Review." And not all items in some nineteenth-century periodicals appear either in the table of contents or the index.

After my review of *Fraser's* and *Blackwood's*, I turned my attention to the *Athenaeum* and the *Academy*. Penzer cites many

Burton letters, articles, and reviews in both of these periodicals; I thought that possibly he and other students of Burton might not have thoroughly examined them. No criticism is intended by this comment—it simply reflects my change in thinking about how and where to find unrecorded Burton material. The *Athenaeum* volumes contain between five hundred and six hundred pages each six-month period, and a satisfactory table of contents does not exist. My review of these two periodicals took several years, on weekends and vacations, and the majority of the unrecorded items I found were discovered in the course of this project.

I did get some assistance from two current sources, *Poole's Index to Periodical Literature, 1802-1906* and *The Wellesley Index to Victorian Periodicals, 1824-1900*. These are both valuable research tools but the number of Burton items recorded in them is minimal. It is worth noting that some nineteenth- and early twentieth-century sources contain information that may be overlooked. Frederick Boase's *Modern English Biography* (1903) cites specific locations in such publications as the *Strand Magazine*, the *Illustrated London News*, and *McCarthy's Portraits of the Sixties*. These sources contain illustrations and information on Isabel. Boase's entry on Richard cites such sources as *Tinsley's Random Recollections, Men of Mark*, the *Illustrated London News*, and *Portraits of Men of Eminence*. Buckland's *Dictionary of Indian Biography* (1906; rpt. 1968) contains brief sketches of the "careers and doings of the large number of persons connected with India, . . . by their exploits, services, and writings." It is curious that while Burton and James Grant are included in this 470-page work there is no entry for John Speke, even though Speke served many years in India and is credited with the discovery of the source of the White Nile. William Crooke's *Hobson-Jobson: A Glossary of Colonial Anglo-Indian Words and Phrases* (1886; rpt. 1969) frequently excerpts Burton's published works for authoritative source material.

Chiefly, however, I relied on my original methods: following up on citations in Burton's own published works and examining periodicals page by page. Following are some examples of unrecorded items that I found.

"Sosivizka, The Bandit of Dalmatia," which appeared in *The Cornhill Magazine* in November 1875 (no. 191, pp. 560-76), is a good example of a Burton work published in a periodical that did not provide the names of contributors. The title alone would not have been sufficient reason for me to connect the article with Burton. The article, which contains some information about the Dalmation seaboard and the people who inhabited it, chiefly chronicles the life and exploits of "Sosivizka," apparently on the basis of an unidentified biography.

Kirkpatrick's catalogue of Burton's library cites this article (item 2110), but the journal and author were not known. Kirkpatrick notes "marked passages" by Richard, and probably by Isabel, too. From this, of course, one could easily have assumed that the article was one Richard kept in his library because it interested him, not because it was one he authored. The *Wellesley Index* makes a tentative attribution of the article to Burton (vol. 1, p. 361). After finding this citation I came across Richard's reference to this article as his own. *The Journal of the Anthropological Institute of Great Britain and Ireland* (1878, vol. 2, p. 343) contains this comment in one of Burton's footnotes: "I have offered a few details concerning the Uzkoks and the Morlaks in 'Sosivizka' etc. (*Cornhill Magazine,* no. 191, November 1875)." My roundabout manner of locating this article confirms an observation recently made by biographers: they point out that too few students of Burton have read enough of his own works.

"Art. V. Afghanistan," in the *Dublin Review* of 1879 (vol. 32, January, pp. 95-119), is an article that may have been written by Richard and Isabel. It contains references to Venice, languages, and geographical locations in Italy, Switzerland, Germany, and France, and advice to the military. Well-known European geographic landmarks are used to characterize similar areas in Afghanistan. Additional comment is provided on rivers, cities, peoples, religions, climate, metals, and roads. Comments demonstrating Richard's interest in Afghanistan are contained in Isabel's *The Life of . . . Burton* (vol. 2, p. 538) and her *Arabia, Egypt, and India* (p. 388). The *Wellesley Index* goes no further than to say that on the basis of records of the *Dublin Review,* this article is "perhaps" a Burton article.

A key source on these matters is Richard's own letters. Several recent Burton biographies have noted that editions of his letters are much needed; the only source of Burton letters with which I am familiar is Don Young's "Selected Correspondence of R. F. Burton" (M.A. thesis, Univ. of Nebraska, 1979). Letters 69 and 76 in this work both contain comments on Richard's interest in Afghanistan and his aspiration to a Foreign Office appointment there. In letter 76, Burton's friend Verney Lovett Cameron writes to Burton and says he wonders whether there is anything to the rumor that Richard is to be appointed consul at Cabul. Greater access to Burton's letters could offer much valuable information on his activities and on his written works.

There are a number of interesting examples of the frequency with which Richard's articles were reprinted, without attribution. In *Every Saturday* magazine, of June and July 1872, Burton's "Damascus" and "Palmyra" were reprinted from *Cassell's Magazine* (1872). *Every Saturday* identified its contents only as "Selected from Foreign Current Literature." The magazine was published in Boston. *Cosmos,* a geographical magazine published in Italy, issued "Midian and the Midianites" in 1878, taken from the *Journal of the Society of Arts* (1878). A large map from Burton's book *The Land of Midian Revisited* accompanied the article. It is probable that Guida Cora, the editor of *Cosmos,* was acquainted with the Burtons. He was an honorary corresponding member of the Royal Geographical Society for years and a professor at the Torino Geographical Institute. (I have left this observation as I originally wrote it in 1990 to illustrate a point: Only in the last few weeks I came across a letter by Richard Burton "To The Editor Of The [London] Times," June

1875. Richard mentions conversing with his "friend . . . Guido Cora of the Cosmos Review." Having at first assumed their friendship I was later able to confirm it.) References to this article in *Cosmos* were found in the *Academy* for December 1878 and for May 1879.

An interesting article authored by Isabel, most likely with Richard's assistance, is "Scenes in Teneriffe." It was published in *Month Magazine* in 1867, in four parts. The parts are subtitled: "Santa Cruz to Oratava," "A Climb Up The Peak," "On The Peak And Down Again," and "Some Account of The Guanches." It comes to twenty-seven pages. In January 1863, the Burtons left England for Madeira, where they spent six weeks. They then sailed to Santa Cruz in Teneriffe and proceeded on to Oratava. The article mentions the English at Teneriffe, yellow fever, the scenery, and the people in general. In the *Life of Burton*, Isabel ended a description of this trip by saying, "Here I wrote my first book on Madeira and Teneriffe; but my husband would not let me print it, because he did not think it was up to the mark" (vol. 1, p. 381). About the end of March, Isabel departed for England and Richard returned to his consulate in Fernando Po, West Africa.

In his biography of Burton, Byron Farwell quotes passages on this trip "from an unpublished book which Isabel wrote on their experiences in the Canary Islands. Richard would not allow her to publish it, saying she needed more practice" (pp. 223-24). Farwell does not give any source for this unpublished "book." Kirkpatrick, in *The Library of Sir R. F. Burton*, cites these four serialized magazine parts. She concludes they were reprinted from an unidentified journal and that they were "probably" by Isabel (item 110, p. 14). Poole's *Index to Periodical Literature* notes an article on this subject but only cites part 1, failing to recognize the remaining three serialized parts. Poole also mistakenly attributes it to Richard.

Isabel's "book" evidently became an article published serially, without authorial attribution. By getting copies of *Month Maga-*

zine through interlibrary loan I was able to see that the article appeared not in one part but four parts and that it was in fact written by Isabel. *Month Magazine* was published from 1864 to 1881, and it is possible that Isabel may have contributed other articles to it. I have not been able to examine the other volumes of this magazine personally. Other articles written by Richard and Isabel will certainly be identified in light of the contents, style, date and supporting documentation from their letters and their known publications.

Periodicals may contain letters by Burton that are also unrecorded. A student of Burton could easily pass over them if the heading or title were the only information available, partly because his interests were so diverse. For example, I would not connect Richard with subjects like "The London Publishing Company," "A Case of Homicide," or "The Proposed Jordan Canal." The page-by-page examination of magazines and journals is often required to establish authorship, even though some topics are more clearly those about which Richard would write. "Kilimanjaro And Its Snows," "African Discoveries," and "The Lakes of Central Africa" are closer to the mark. A few of these letters in combination sometimes convey a fairly complete picture of Richard's thoughts on a topic.

In the *Athenaeum* for 19 July 1862, Richard writes from Fernando Po to answer Petermann and Cooley letters about Mt. Kilimanjaro. In letters written between 8 February and 8 March 1862, Petermann and Cooley debated the question of the impetus for the Burton and Speke expedition to the Central African lake region. Petermann credits the East African Mombas missionaries, Krapf, Rebmann, and Erhardt, with stimulating their interest. Cooley cites prior motivations back to 1835. He is also convinced that there could be no "perpetual snow" atop Mt. Kilimanjaro because it is near the equator. Cooley adds that the Royal Geographical Society gave Burton "misinformation" and restrained his "inquiry and freedom of speech."

On 19 July 1862, Burton responded that he had never tried to reach Kilimanjaro. His orders were to explore the Sea of Unyamwezi. Preparatory to departing for the interior, he made a trip to Fuga, where Mr. and Mrs. Rebmann lived, a visit mentioned in the *Atheneum* for 28 November 1857. Their lives were saved, despite warring Wamasai, because of this trip, Burton contends. He denies that any restraints were placed on him by the Royal Geographical Society and affirms that the "intense cold" and the height of Kilimanjaro justify reports of snow. Richard concludes with a characteristic statement that is part humor and part serious challenge. He says that he believes that Mt. Kilimanjaro is topped with snow and if Her Majesty's Government could be induced to send him, he would return with "a Bottle of Kilimanjarian snow."

In "African Discoveries," published in the *Athenaeum,* 18 June 1864, Richard responds to letters from John Speke (23 January 1864) and Charles Beke (30 January 1864). It is Speke's position that the Mombas missionaries, Rebmann and Erhardt, had inspired the 1858 Burton-Speke expedition that led to the discovery of Lake Victoria. Speke asserts that Burton "feared" to take a direct line to the interior and that he taught Burton the geography of the countries they traversed. Beke argues that in 1846 he was alone in pointing out that the "sources of the Nile lay west of Zanzibar." He proposes a third expedition to complement those of Burton and Speke. Beke defends Burton and attempts to discredit Speke. In his response to these letters, Burton challenges Speke's statement that fear guided him in the choice of the line of march and points out that the Mombas missionary map was inaccurate. This map soon came to be called the "Slug Map" because it combined two lakes, Nyassa and Tanganyika, in a slug-like configuration. Burton criticizes Speke's description of the lake region and declares that Victoria Nyanza is a "huge lagoon" fed by a number of streams. He closes with another of his characteristic flourishes, urging that future explorers of the Nile source not return with "such a maximum of 'cry' and a minimum of 'wool'" as did Speke.

This controversy over the Nile source is of course further documented in recorded letters and books included in Penzer.

Another unrecorded Burton letter appears in the *Athenaeum* for 11 December 1875. Speke had died in 1864 and Burton here addresses James Grant, who accompanied Speke on his return expedition to Lake Victoria. Burton contradicts statements Grant made in a paper presented before the Royal Geographical Society on how long the Central African lakes had been known to geographers. He addresses an issue first raised elsewhere, Speke's inability to communicate with Arab traders because he did not understand Arabic. Burton brings up another longstanding complaint against Speke, who had not kept his promise to wait for Burton's return from their 1858 expedition before reporting to the Royal Geographical Society. Speke, of course, had gone to the Society without Burton, thereby enhancing his chances of becoming the leader of the return expedition to establish the Nile source. Burton credits himself with being the first to "*prove* that 'the centre of Africa is studded with lakes'—is a lake region to the fullest extent of the term."

A recitation of unrecorded Burton letters, articles, reviews, official reports, and miscellaneous items and ephemera should not be an end in itself. From a growing body of published and unpublished material, we should seek to broaden our understanding of the motivations and activities of Richard and Isabel Burton. I have described my approach to the discovery of unrecorded but published Burton items in this paper, but the quest for never-published material should not be overlooked. Some evidence of never-published material can be gleaned from the 1976 Spink and Son sale catalogue, which contained a large number of Burton books. In addition, there were manuscripts, sketches in Richard's hand, official government reports, and what appeared to be background material for unpublished works. Certainly there are some of these items in the hands of private collectors, occasionally even made available to the public, as was Burton's *Uruguay*, probably completed in the early 1870s and finally published in 1982, using the Huntington Library manuscript (HM 27954). It appears that the footnotes to the manuscript may be in the hands of a private collector and they remain unpublished. The Huntington Library has recently published an edition based on its manuscript of lectures that Burton originally delivered in Brazil, *Sir Richard Burton's Travels in Arabia and Africa: Four Lectures from a Huntington Library Manuscript* (1990).

Based on my work with magazines, journals, and newspapers, I wish to make some general observations. In addition to writing letters and articles on scientific topics, current events, and literary matters, Burton kept up a constant flow of correspondence to editors detailing his explorations, his mining endeavors, the writing and publication of his books, and his concerns about military and political events. This correspondence provoked dozens of entries in periodicals, under generic headings like "Scientific Notice," "Review," "Our Library." My belief is that this trail of documentation and observation represents more than just Burton's unflagging drive to write and to correspond. It was also his intent to promote himself and his activities. He wished it to be known among those with power and influence that he was involved, informed, and ready to serve if called upon. His efforts to discover gold and other minerals were well reported. The types of mineral ores and their volume were described. It was most likely Burton's intention to offer these detailed notices prior to the actual laboratory test results in order to build up a favorable public disposition to invest in his ventures.

It seems to me that many students of Burton's life paint him as so uncompromising in his ideals that he undermined his own efforts to advance. But as inspection reports confirm, he had been motivated to be a successful East Indian Company Army officer, and his study of languages was rewarded with extra pay (India Office Library and Records, L/MIL/12/73). His career in the foreign service reached a pinnacle when he was appointed to the Damascus consulate in 1869. He worked hard at searching for precious metals and at writing, though neither endeavor led to financial reward. His single profitable venture was his sixteen-volume *Arabian Nights*. I think we can acknowledge a pragmatic and ambitious Burton who clearly recognized that mere honest endeavor in public service was seldom sufficient to bring acclaim or anything more than modest financial security. But he unfortunately offered his talents to a public not prone to recognize excellence or unconventional achievement. Overall, I think, he was willing to let future generations judge him and his endeavors.

L. P. Kirwan, in his "Meditations on the Burton Mausoleum at Mortlake," in the *Geographical Journal* for 1975, has said: "Most of the great nineteenth-century explorers . . . have become somewhat statuesque figures. Revered but remote from our contemporary scene, they remain firmly fixed in the Victorian era. But perhaps because he was such a perplexed (and is such a perplexing) man, Burton has remained a remarkably contemporary character" (p. 49). It is as our contemporary that we address Burton at this conference. We wait with anticipation for his next letter, article, or review. We marvel at his addressing a subject we did not anticipate. We hope for the next and more comprehensive study of his life and for the footnote that reveals another of his thoughts. Throughout his writing, regardless of type or genre, Burton intended to be heard beyond his own time. As we read Burton's works and search for additional items, he speaks to us over the distances. He is in motion once again.

Gorilla-hunting, from Burton's copy of Paul B. Du Chaillu's *Explorations and Adventures in Equatorial Africa* (1861; Burton Library 1558).

Burton and His Library

by Alan H. Jutzi

In her foreword to *The Life of Captain Sir Richard F. Burton,* Isabel Burton observed, "Richard was such a many-sided man, he will have appeared different to every set of people who knew him. . . . Loads of books will be written about him, and every one will be different" (1893 edition, 1:xi). Indeed, since then every serious biographical study of Burton has resulted in a slightly altered view of this baffling man.

A survey of Burton's own library reveals the many and diverse sides of Burton. It shows him as a man endowed with extraordinary mental abilities and imbued with insatiable curiosity, a man who demanded intellectual honesty and who was driven by a tenacious ethic of "work, work, work." An analysis of his library will tell us how a London journalist was led to make this apparently hyperbolic claim about Burton: "While the best of ordinary men never aspire to know more than something of everything, and everything of something, [Burton] might almost without exaggeration be said to know everything of everything" (I. Burton, *Life of Burton,* 2:269).

In this talk I will concentrate primarily on Burton as writer, scholar, and linguist. We will see the opinionated Burton, who hated religious cant, exposed blatant falsehood, and railed against governmental and institutional incompetence. In the tattered tomes of his library can also be found a more personal

Burton, the man who readily befriended scholars and writers and developed strong intellectual attachments, yet exhibited fierce animosity toward his enemies Finally, we will consider Burton as a critic—questioning, correcting, refining, and defining.

Few personal libraries are so revealing. But merely knowing which books comprise Burton's library does not tell us much: it is Burton's practice of annotating books and of filling them with personal papers that allows us to analyze Burton's response to what he was reading and to ascertain how he used his books. A survey of his library leads one to conclude that Burton began making notes in books regularly at least as early as the mid-1840s, when he was in India. Thereafter nearly every book he read (with the exception of works of fiction) bears some markings. From all evidence, he could not even browse through a book without a pen or pencil in hand; he was an addicted critic.

Burton made many different kinds of notes, but there are a few distinctive short ones that appear repeatedly in the outer margins and seem to have become his standard catchwords. Going from the most complimentary to the most derogatory they are as follows: "true" means of course that he agreed; "good" might refer either to content or expression; "NB" indicates he thought something worth remembering; "eh" and "oh" are disparaging, roughly equivalent to "is this possible?" "No," of course, suggests his view that a statement was incorrect; "rot" was a shorter equivalent of several acerbic phrases which he also used at times, "complete falsehood," "an horrendous lie," "a gross exaggeration," or "dribble." In some cases Burton kept up a running commentary in the margins, employing these single descriptive words, with other equally pointed phrases occasionally thrown in.

A good example of Burton's technique appears in Paul Du Chaillu's *Exploration and Adventures in Equatorial Africa* (Burton Library 155; henceforward "BL"). Du Chaillu was a friend of Burton's, celebrated at the time for exhibiting mounted African gorilla specimens in Europe and America. Burton's marginal comments in chapter seven, where Du Chaillu first reports seeing a gorilla, provide a marvelous introduction to his unique style of annotation. Du Chaillu writes, "Suddenly Miengai uttered a little *cluck* with his tongue, which is the native's way of showing that something is stirring, and that a sharp look-out is necessary. [Burton scrawls "true" next to that line.] And presently I noticed, ahead of us seemingly, a noise as of some one breaking down branches or twigs. . . . We walked with the greatest care, making no noise at all. The countenances of the men showed that they thought themselves engaged in a very serious undertaking; but we push on. . . . [Burton writes "Bah!" with an exclamation point next to that sentence.] Then the underbrush swayed rapidly ahead, and presently before us stood an immense male gorilla. . . . Nearly six feet high with immense body, huge chest, and great muscular arms, with fiercely-glaring large deep gray eyes, and a hellish expression of face, which seemed to me like some nightmare vision: thus stood before us this king of the African forest. [That drew a "nonsense" from Burton.] He was not afraid of us. He stood there, and beat his breast with his huge fists till it resounded like an immense bass-drum, which is their mode of offering defiance; meantime giving vent to roar after roar." In one margin Burton writes "I don't believe this"; in the other, "natives say they rise to attack." The account continues, "The roar of the gorilla is the most singular and awful noise heard in these African woods. It begins with a sharp *bark,* like an angry dog, then glides into a deep bass *roll,* which literally and closely resembles the roll of distant thunder along the sky, for which I have sometimes been tempted to take it where I did not see the animal." This last line elicited a "hoo, hoo, hoo" (BL 1558, pp. 70-71).

Before considering other individual works, we should take a look at the tragic history of the library. The first catastrophe occurred at Grindley's London warehouse in 1861, where nearly all of Burton's books were lost in a fire together with his collection of Persian and Arabic manuscripts and Asian

88 *In Search of Sir Richard Burton*

Suddenly Miengai uttered a little *cluck* with his tongue, which is the native's way of showing that something is stirring, and that a sharp look-out is necessary. And presently I noticed, ahead of us seemingly, a noise as of some one breaking down branches or twigs of trees.

This was the gorilla, I knew at once, by the eager and satisfied looks of the men. They looked once more carefully at their guns, to see if by any chance the powder had fallen out of the pans; I also examined mine, to make sure that all was right; and then we marched on cautiously.

The singular noise of the breaking of tree-branches continued. We walked with the greatest care, making no noise at all. The countenances of the men showed that they thought themselves engaged in a very serious undertaking; but we pushed on, until finally we thought we saw through the thick woods the moving of the branches and small trees which the great beast was tearing down, probably to get from them the berries and fruits he lives on.

Suddenly, as we were yet creeping along, in a silence which made a heavy breath seem loud and distinct, the woods were at once filled with the tremendous barking roar of the gorilla.

Then the underbrush swayed rapidly just ahead, and presently before us stood an immense male gorilla. He had gone through the jungle on his all-fours; but when he saw our party he erected himself and looked us boldly in the face. He stood about a dozen yards from us, and was a sight I think I shall never forget. Nearly six feet high (he proved four inches shorter), with immense body, huge chest, and great muscular arms, with fiercely-glaring large deep gray eyes, and a hellish expression of face, which seemed to me like some nightmare vision: thus stood before us this king of the African forest.

He was not afraid of us. He stood there, and beat his breast with his huge fists till it resounded like an immense bass-drum, which is their mode of offering defiance; meantime giving vent to roar after roar.

The roar of the gorilla is the most singular and awful noise heard in these African woods. It begins with a sharp *bark*, like an angry dog, then glides into a deep bass *roll*, which literally

Burton's annotations to Paul B. Du Chaillu's *Explorations and Adventures in Equatorial Africa,* p. 70.

costumes. The fire destroyed books Burton may have saved from his youth; books that he acquired for Oxford; texts used to learn Hindostani, Persian, Arabic, and other languages that Burton asssimilated in India; Arabic books consulted for his pilgrimage to Mecca; and most of the volumes he employed in preparing for his expedition to Harar and for his exploration of the lake region of Central Africa.

What specific books did succumb to the Grindley flames? Possibly a tattered edition of *Pickwick,* along with French and Italian stories that enthralled the young Burton, and from his student days the Kabbalah, which recent biographer Edward Rice maintains influenced Burton when he was at Oxford. To that mystic text should be added the occult writings of Cornelius Agrippa, Thomas Erpenius's Arabic grammar, as well as Duncan Forbes's Hindostani grammar. The East India Company standard issues would probably have been kept by Burton: Wellington's *Dispatches,* the Army regulations, and Mill's ponderous *History of India* (see I. Burton, *Life of Burton,* 1:95, 153). Hindu religious texts, Persian literary and philosophical works, a large collection of linguistic books, a diverse collection of erotica, and Jacob Burckhardt's *Travels in Arabia* would probably have been housed at Grindley. Almost all of the books that motivated and inspired young Burton and that he consulted in his most productive years as an explorer and writer are gone.

By the time Alfred Bates Richards visited the Burtons in Trieste in the 1880s, the library had been replenished with an estimated six thousand volumes. Isabel's figure was eight thousand. In their first Trieste home, every one of the small rooms of the house contained shelves of books, memorabilia, and collectibles. In their second home, along the walls of Burton's large study were books organized by subject categories and by topics on which he was currently working (see Alfred Bates Richards, *A Sketch of the Career of Richard F. Burton,* 1886, p. 34).

There is a reprint in Burton's library entitled *The Destruction of Libraries by Fire considered practically and historically,* by Cornelius

Walford (BL 269). Walford begins his treatise with this statement: "The destruction of libraries, whether large or small, public or private, is always an event deeply to be deplored: not simply on the ground of intrinsic value of the objects consumed, but because, too often, the treasures destroyed cannot be replaced by mere pecuniary outlay, and frequently not at all." Burton could not have known that the Grindley fire would not be the only conflagration to affect his library.

After his death Isabel Burton spent sixteen days sifting through his papers and library. She then burned the manuscript of the infamous "Scented Garden" and his journals and diaries. At the same time she probably destroyed all of Burton's correspondence and papers related to the publications of the Kama Shastra Society as well as the Kama Shastra publications themselves, excepting *The Arabian Nights*. She sterilized the book collection, removing anything that could possibly be construed as erotic or pornographic—actually anything with sexual information. This also meant the burning of a large file of letters from scholars and collectors and a second file of collected "sexual" literature in manuscript. There is only one example presently surviving in his library of the kind of regular exchanges that Burton carried on with friends interested in the subject (see BL 2010).

During this same period she decided to weed out other sections of his library. All of the fiction was extracted and probably sold to a bookseller. There is only a handful of fiction in his library today and the titles appear to be Isabel's favorites, not Richard's. It is likely that Isabel did not consider these books part of his "working" library, for she reports how Richard read entertaining literature in the evening to relax. Norman Penzer, Burton's first bibliographer, believed that Isabel disposed of the more valuable and collectible books through Bernard Quaritch, but I have been unable to verify this from Quaritch catalogs distributed between 1890 and 1896 or from the records of the firm itself.

All told Isabel shipped back 204 boxes of books, papers, and memorabilia of her husband's in the spring of 1891. According to Norman Penzer, Mrs. Fitzgerald, Isabel's sister, and a friend, Minnie Grace Plowman, became Isabel's literary executors upon her death in March 1896. Mrs. Fitzgerald "wanted to burn all the mss. and books," but they were saved by Miss Plowman. She contacted Herbert Jones, librarian of the Central Library, Kensington, who agreed to accept the Burton Library. A small bequest of Richard and Isabel Burton's publications and memorabilia had been given by Isabel to the Camberwell Vestry; this is now deposited in the Richmond-upon-Thames Library (see Norman Penzer, *An Annotated Bibliography of Sir Richard Francis Burton*, 1923, pp. 291-93).

In 1896 the Kengsington Library made a handwritten list of items (now at the Huntington) in Burton's library, and from that first record one can calculate that over one hundred and sixty titles are no longer among his books. The destruction caused by a severe flood in the basement of the library after World War II, I believe, accounts for most of this loss. Charles Darwin's *Journal of Researches into Natural History of the Countries Visited during the Voyage of the H.M.S. Beagle* (1860) and *On the Origin of Species* (1861) are the most important of these missing books. Because Darwin's theories played such a significant role in shaping Burton's anthropological views, it would have been extremely valuable to see his marginal comments in these copies.

In 1955 the Burton Library went to the Royal Anthropological Institute, where a major effort was made to restore the ravaged collection. In 1978 B. J. Kirkpatrick's catalog of the library was published. Although the index is unreliable, this detailed catalog provides today the only real access to Burton's library. In 1986 the Royal Anthropological Institute, under severe financial pressure, sold the entire Burton Library to the late Allan Christensen and the Christensen Fund, which deposited it in the Huntington Library.

Burton's library today contains about twenty-seven hundred books and pamphlets, one hundred maps, several hundred letters written to Burton, manuscripts of Burton's published works, research notes amassed by Burton for additional volumes of his *Book of the Sword*, and his translation of the Hindustani version of Pilpay's fables, done in 1847.

In writing about British book collectors, Bernard Quaritch maintained that "most of the works required by Burton during his varied career were provided by, and on the advice of, Mr. Quaritch" (Bernard Quaritch, ed., *Towards A Dictionary of English Book Collectors, 1892-1921*). Athough Burton undoubtedly purchased many books from the Quaritch firm, mostly Arabic and Oriental texts and translations, in buying books Burton usually relied on local proprietors—much in the same spirit that he lived, dressed, ate, and spoke like the natives. When it was impossible to find a book nearby, however, he would not hesitate to contact friends, booksellers, or publishers to locate a much-needed text.

When he was in South America as consul in Santos, Burton relied heavily on the bookshop of Garraux de Lailhacar in San Paulo. In Trieste he bought from Schimpff's Buchhandlung, and when he needed to rebuild his collection after the Grindley tragedy he received the assistance of many book people, including Paternoster bookseller Edward Cowell, who hunted down editions of Hafiz, the Persian lyrical poet. Burton seems to have rummaged through bookshops with the same exhaustive thoroughness with which he explored the world's libraries and museums.

Burton was also given many books by friends and admiring associates, particularly late in his life when he devoted much of his time to translating and book reviewing. He built friendships with fellow scholars everywhere; he relied on expert assistance, at the same time readily returning favors. These colleagues presented books to Burton: Edward H. Palmer, the Trinity College Orientalist who suffered a horrible death at the hand of the Bedouin; I. V. Cameron, a younger man but Burton's closest exploring associate; linguist R. S. Charnock; and F. F. Arbuthnot, co–publisher and conspirator in the Kama Shastra Society.

On at least two occasions Burton received not only a copy of the work but a flattering printed dedication. Folklorist W. A. Clouston honored his friend in his book *Popular Tales and Fictions, Their Migrations and Transformations*: "To Sir Richard F. Burton K.C.M.G., the eminent scholar and world-wide traveller; whose notes to his complete translation of 'The Book of the Thousand Nights and a Night' are ample evidence of his interest in, and knowledge of, the Genealogy of popular tales; these volumes are dedicated by the Author" (BL 823).

One of the most delightful presentations came from Justin Huntly McCarthy, a promising young writer then also a member of Parliament: "May a young & humble student of all things oriental be permitted to lay at the feet of the greatest master of Eastern thought & Eastern life the first fruits of his studies in the form of the little volume of verse called 'Hafiz in London' which goes to you by this past post" (BL 932). McCarthy became very close to the elderly Burtons, so much so that it was a McCarthy poem that Isabel affixed to Richard's mausoleum at Mortlake.

The only book gift from Isabel to Richard that I have been able to identify was J. F. Schoen's *Oku Ibo: Grammatical Elements of the Ibo Language* (BL 504). It was given on "Easter Sunday 1862." Such an esoteric present on a sacred Christian holiday implies much about Richard's preferences, and perhaps about the couple's inexplicable relationship as well.

Burton was not a book collector; he had little interest in the bibliographical features or the preciousness of books. They were to be probed and digested, and few students have been as assiduous in their pursuit of knowledge as Burton. Isabel gave us the best description of how Burton read and worked. When Alfred Bates Richards visited their home in Trieste, his puzzled expression drew this response from her: "I see you are looking at our tables. Everyone does. Dick likes a separate table for every book, and when he is tired of one he goes to another" (Richards, *A Sketch of the Career*, p. 34). In her biography she recalled Burton's study habits:

> In *early* life he studied everything till he had passed in it. . . .
> In after life he kept his knowledge on a steady platform,
> studying up all things. . . . He never passed a day without
> reading up something in one of his twenty-nine lan-
> guages. . . . He then read a good deal, and took notes, and
> cut any interesting paragraphs from about ten English
> and four local papers. . . . He used to examine into the
> meaning and the etymology of words as he went on, with
> all their bearings and different spellings; he never read
> hurriedly, passing anything over. He wrote for a certain
> time in the day at several tables—a table to each work. He
> kept himself up in all the passing events of the day, wrote
> his journal, copied anything that struck him, and at night
> he always 'cooled his head' with a novel. (I. Burton, *Life of
> Burton,* 2:260)

Excepting her inaccurate impression that Burton kept up all twenty-nine languages, this is a fair description of how Burton worked the last seventeen years of his life.

There are many examples of the in-depth study that Burton could give to any one topic—probably the best can be found in the extensive files on the sword and the manuscripts and notes for translating Camoens, now in the Edwards H. Metcalf Collection—but the clearest demonstration of how Burton could "attack" a book appears in the *Makamat or Rhetorical Anecdotes of Al Harari of Basra* (BL 910). Burton's chaotic scribble in this volume indicates his complete preoccupation with Al Harari's formal and elegant Arabic poetic style; his cramped pencil scrawl, frequently difficult to decipher, confirms that Burton was as interested in the classical, refined tradition in Arabic literature as he was in the bawdy folk tales of *The Arabian Nights*.

Burton's reading reflects prodigious endurance and tenacity. A significant number of books are annotated from beginning to end. He made his way through the entire four-volume edition of Ibn Khallikan's *Biographical Dictionary of the Moslem People* (BL 126), published in Paris between 1842 and 1871, as well as the entire 677 pages of Parkhurst's *A Hebrew and English Lexicon, without Points; in which the Hebrew and Chaldee Words of the Old Testament Are Explained* (BL 544). Of the sixty volumes he owned of the Hakluyt Society exploration series, he read nearly all; the Bohn Classical series has notes in about half of the eighty volumes.

Of course, Burton's reading was not always so demanding. He frequently depended on unsophisticated works to provide him with basic information. *A History of the United States of America* (BL 1724), published in Boston for high-school level students, served as an introduction to the United States. He was not above consulting such elementary compendiums as *Rudiments of Geology* (BL 1327), published by William and Robert Chambers. He carried around and relied on popular guidebooks of all kinds, even one for Niagara Falls (BL 1730).

A survey of his entire library, first of all, gives us a composite picture of Burton's inquisitive nature and the diversity of his interests. These are the categories in which his library is now organized: anthropology, archeology, and folklore; biography; geography and travel; linguistics; literature (including the Greek and Roman classics); medicine and psychology; religion and philosophy; the sciences—natural and applied; the sword; Africa, North and South America, Asia, and Europe. Burton was only limited by the extent of his own curiosity—and that was nearly infinite. There are very few libraries in the world—private or public—which include copies of *Phrenology Made Practical and Popular* (BL 1119), William Charles Wells's *Essay on Dew* (BL 1404), and *The Twenty-second Annual Report of the Managing Committee of the Kurrachee Municipal Library and Museum* (BL 2008). Handwritten notes provide evidence that Burton actually read these books.

Second, Burton's marginalia show that he was a remarkable observer, obsessed with comparing what he witnessed with what others recorded in print. His geographical and ethnographic books are filled with penciled responses to the author's observations. Two examples illustrate this point. Horn's *Overland Guide, from the U.S. Indian Sub-Agency, Council Bluff... to the City of Sacramento* (BL 1729) was a popular guide to the American West's overland route during the mid-nineteenth century. Burton took it along as he crossed the continent and jotted down short notes next to Horn's brief descriptions. Burton recorded the dates as they arrived at various locations and commented here and there about the conditions of the route. Of the journey along the Platte River he wrote, "Red Hills horrid place"; or of Fort Hall, a key stopping point, "Fort is dead place." One ocean away, in the southern hemisphere, Burton compares his own experiences in the Congo with descriptions in *A Narrative of an Expedition to Explore the River Zaire usually called the Congo, in South Africa, in 1816* (BL 1689). Burton's impressions of the flora and fauna on the river were entirely different, judging from the great frequency of the marginal comment "none now."

Third, Burton's library confirms his fascination with what today are the fields of comparative philology, anthropology, and folk literature. His library reflects not only his abiding love of Arab culture but the appeal that many other ethnic, linquistic, and national groups held for him. His incessant traveling and exploration went hand in hand with an energetic intellectual scrutiny of the people and places he contacted. Very few Englishman traveling in the British Empire shared Burton's desire to understand and appreciate the Empire's cultural diversity. In fact, he had a consuming interest in a multitude of diverse cultures.

Burton's practice of inserting letters, manuscripts, drawings, hand-drawn maps, newspaper and magazine clippings, and printed ephemera of all kinds often provides valuable insights into his activities and his reading of a text. Among the pages of some volumes can be found unpublished and largely unidentified pieces. There are at least two handwritten itineraries, or journal fragments, from his rather mysterious 1860 trip to the

United States. In a tourist pamphlet entitled "The Tomb of Washington at Mt. Vernon" (BL 1759) is an incomplete note on his visit to Mt. Vernon. Ten leaves from his daily journal covering 19 October to 23 October 1860, just after he left Salt Lake City, are pasted in his own copy of *The City of the Saints* (BL 11).

Burton was an inveterate sketcher. A pencil drawing of Le Plateau, the French capital of Gabon, is stuck in one of the many bound pamphlet volumes in his library. But the most important collection of Burton sketches appears in the first pages of his copy of *The Lake Regions of Central Africa* (BL 10). These crude drawings of natives and camp scenes are indicative of the kind of sketch that Burton must have executed in his journals on a daily basis while he was traveling.

Bound into the 1816 historical narrative of a trip down the Congo River just mentioned is the only scientific manuscript in his library from his African explorations, a meterological record he kept for September 1863. Burton was a competent field cartographer. A rather unsophisticated but intriguing example was found folded into his copy of David Livingstone's *Missionary Travels and Researches in South Africa* (BL 1622). Burton entitled it, "Diagram to assist in the reading of Dr. Livingstone's letter. Bangweolo July 8, 1868." This was apparently an attempt to figure out Livingstone's route through southeastern Africa.

A most delightful newsclipping I discovered is pasted in the front of Burton's *Abeokuta and the Cameroons Mountains* (BL 13). It actually was a report on a failed meeting of the Royal Geographical Society:

> "A vast and very uncomfortable crowd attended the Section of Ethnology, to hear Captain Burton's paper on 'The Ascent of the Congo River.' But there is a fate about this paper. Already postponed twice, it was to-day again necessarily postponed, because the map necessary to describe the route was at the theatre, where it would have to be put up for Dr. Livingstone's lecture to-night. The audience had a great notion of being angry when Sir

Roderick made the announcement; but when, after Captain Burton explained the absoluteness of the necessity, and Mrs. Captain Burton, by his side, looked an appeal, the audience became smiling and applauded."

The few books from Burton's early career which escaped the fire at Grindley tell us a great deal about how he used and valued his library. Two Marathi texts studied by Burton in India in the mid-1840s disclose a story that bears telling in its entirety (BL 1958). The story can be pieced together from letters accompanying the two volumes. In 1876 Richard returned to India, with Isabel, and while in Bombay he received a letter from Bapoojee Hurree Scindia, a clerk from the Booldana district in Hyderabad. He wrote:

> Most respected Sir, When you get this letter, you will no doubt be very much surprised at it; but when I explain to you who I am, your surprise will wear away, and then you will bring to mind one whom you have perhaps long forgotten, but who is ever remembering you with most grateful remembrances.—Now in order to introduce myself to you, I shall endeavour to recall such events as will assist in bringing me to your kind recollection.—
>
> It was in 1854, that you had taken up your quarters at the house of the Honorable J. G. Lumsden, then member of the Bombay Government Council. It was at that place and in that year that I was so fortunate as to become acquainted with you. Mr. Lumsden used to live then at the "Belair" on the Mazagoonside of the island.—you had then with you an African servant named "Salmin," and an Arab butler, whose name I have now forgotten.—you had then returned from your tour of exploration to Mecca and were writing the work called "Pilgrimage to Mecca & Medina."—I used to Copy from your manuscript such portions as you gave me, as you said that my writing was good for that purpose.—This work was afterwards pub-

lished but I have never seen it except in advertisements.

You were good enough to give me (present) a number of Mahratta and English books.—all of which I have now in my possession. Your own remarks and notes on the margin of the Mahratta books are very dear to me, and I often read them, in order to think of you.

In another letter written a few days later he added:

The notes on the history of the Mahrattas are the ones which I often read, and show to others, as something wonderful, coming from the pen of a European gentleman.— Because it is seldom that a European can write with so much correctness and ease, a language entirely [a] stranger to him.

Burton must have been ecstatic to hear about the survival of these two books, for shortly thereafter he asked Bapoojee to bring them to Bombay. In exchange for the return of his gift, Burton presented to his former copyist his *Personal Narrative of a Pilgrimage to El-Medinah and Meccah*. At Bapoojee's request he also provided him with a chit as a personal reference. Although Isabel asserted several times in print that Richard shrugged off the loss of his first library, in this instance he jumped at the chance to recover some small portion of it.

The incident with Bapoojee and the Marathi books illustrates another Burton idiosyncrasy—his small and nearly unreadable handwriting. This was the first time, as far as I am aware, that Burton employed an amanuensis, and it was probably during or shortly after his Mecca pilgrimage that his handwriting began to deteriorate significantly. (Because of the need for secrecy in Arabia he may have trained himself to fit a reduced script onto smaller pieces of paper.) We can only speculate about why the style and size of his lettering changed, but there is certainly evidence that the transformation, from India to East Africa, was dramatic. In the Marathi work *History of the Marat* his writing is large and readable; his notes in books used in East Africa display a hand that has become smaller, flatter, and less legible.

There are four other books from the Indian-Sind period (1842-48) that I have been able to identify. Burton purchased a Portuguese dictionary in Bombay in 1843, probably in anticipation of his trip to Goa (BL 650). In 1844 he bought a 1652 edition of Virgil's works (BL 1084). In Karachi in 1845 he acquired the *Travels of Ibn Batuta*, a fourteenth-century narrative taken from an Arabic manuscript in the Cambridge Public Library and published by the Oriental Translation Society (BL 1993). It seems logical to assume that his library at the time included many similar works. The only grammar from this period when Burton was so preoccupied with the study of languages is a copy of John Richardson's *A Grammar of the Arabic Language* (BL 551). It is uncertain how these books escaped the flames at Grindley.

Burton returned from India in poor health, and appropriately enough two extant works concern medicine. Weiss's *Handbook of Hydropathy* was a book meticulously examined, for in the front Burton laid out the daily cold-water regimen he underwent between 18 May and 3 July 1852 (BL 1178). This treatment may have been undertaken with medical supervision, for on the title page the name of Dr. Ellis Sudbrooke Park, Richmond on Surrey, appears. The other work is a pamphlet entitled *The Movement Cure*—a health guide which sounds like it might be a current best-seller in Southern California (BL 1134). The author states that his ideas and methods come from the Swedish poet and gymnasiarch Henry Ling and that the "movement-cure consists of a methodical application of well-defined and appropriate rhythmical movements to the human body." Burton apparently adopted some of these techniques, for he lists gymnastic moves such as side-bending, twisting, and stooping. There are a few more books preserved in Burton's library from his exploring period in East Africa (1854-59) than from his early

Indian career. In his *Lake Regions of Central Africa* Burton spends a long chapter on the provisions, equipment, clothing, and books which he took on his expedition. Of the seventeen books in the inventory seven remain. Pritchard's *Natural History of Man* (BL 294) and Cuvier's *The Animal Kingdom* (BL 273) served him as scientific reference works. Their size was apparently not a consideration, for both of them are bulky volumes. Norie's work on navigation and Gordon's *Lunar and Time Tables* (BL 1356) were practical exploring tools. But the most utilitarian choices were Colonel J. R. Jackson's *What to Observe: or, the Traveller's Remembrancer* (BL 426), Sir Francis Galton's *The Art of Travel* (BL 381), and Johannes L. Krapf's *Kisuáheli Language* (BL 484). Jackson and Galton attempted to answer the questions, what does an explorer need to know before setting off; what should he take along; and what information does he need to interpret what he sees? From Burton's comments in these books one can assume he consulted them not only when preparing for his expedition but during his travel and later when writing *Lake Regions*. In the Jackson volume, Burton seems to have read the chapters on geography, meteorology, geology, instruments, and operations. In the front of the Galton, Burton wrote, "This excellent book requires a long appendix," and then he outlined what he would have added. As with many other books, Burton created his own index on the front flyleaf; he also redrew some of Galton's engravings and in the margins revised or augmented many of Galton's suggestions. From this book alone one would conclude that Burton took an enormous load of equipment and supplies on his central African expedition.

Burton's notes in Krapf's *Kisuáheli Language* provide us with a splendid example of the techniques he used to master quickly a new and difficult language. Burton's ability to learn a language and his facility with many languages is legendary. This is Burton's own explanation of how he could "break the neck" of a language in two months:

> I got a simple grammar and vocabulary, marked out the forms and words which I knew were absolutely necessary, and learnt them by heart by carrying them in my pocket and looking over them at spare moments during the day. I never worked for more than a quarter of an hour at a time, for after that the brain lost its freshness. After learning some three hundred words, easily done in a week, I stumbled through some easy book-work (one of the Gospels is the most come-atable), and underlined every word that I wished to recollect, in order to read over my pencillings at least once a day. Having finished my volume, I then carefully worked up the grammar minutiae, and I then chose some other book whose subject most interested me. The neck of the language was now broken, and progress was rapid. (I. Burton, *Life of Burton*, 1:80)

In the first few leaves of Krapf's grammar, Burton has written down the key words and laid out the simple structure of the declensions and conjugations. From this simplified beginning he progressed until he learned how to converse in Swaheli. Although Burton was extremely critical of Christian missionaries in Africa, he relied heavily on vocabularies and grammars published by missionary societies, as well as on the knowledge of such explorer-missionaries as Krapf. Two other African languages studied by Burton were Yoruba and Mpongwe, and at least one of them was not so easily learned. He gave a succinct critique of Yoruba in the grammar, "Hard to write and Pronounce. Almost inaudible initial vowels & terminal nazels. Presence of accents as Chinese, rise & fall of voice. Great volubility and archaisms" (BL 470).

From the presence of books on African exploration in Burton's library one can infer that he was actively involved to the very end in the Nile controversy. All the key antagonists and explorers are represented: Krapf, W. D. Cooley, Charles Beke, James Grant, Samuel Baker, David Livingstone, V. L. Cameron, Henry Stanley, and, of course, John Hanning Speke. The annotations in Burton's books not only disclose his opinions of the chief players but also reveal his unbridled bitterness toward the prime culprit, John Hanning Speke.

Scattered in the margins of works by Krapf, Cooley, and Baker are Burton's responses, tearing to shreds nonsensical observations and overblown conclusions. This statement about the English character from Baker's *The Albert N'Yanza* received Burton's angry "rot:" "The English," Baker declared, "are as English in Australia, India, and America, as they are in England, and in every locality they exhibit the industry and energy of their native land" (BL 1507). Although Burton questioned Henry Stanley's accuracy, a marginal "good" appears here and there in the four Stanley works in his library (BL 1681-84). It was for Livingstone and Speke that he saved his most stinging and spiteful remarks.

The gulf between Burton and Livingstone, clearly reflected in Burton's notes, was a consequence of his disdain of Livingstone's Christian missionary beliefs. Time and again he attacks his dogmatism. Early in Livingstone's *Missionary Travels and Researches in South Africa,* Livingstone exclaimed: "The command to 'go into all the world and preach the gospel to every creature' must be obeyed by Christians either personally or by substitute" (BL 1622, p. 34). "Rot" was Burton's consistent and characteristic response to this and similar passages.

Occasionally in his annotations Burton divulged some intriguing or privileged information. In the introduction to this same work Livingstone wrote that "several friends" suggested that he make his account personal and write about himself. Next to this paragraph Burton noted, "R. Murchison suggested this, which sold the book" (p. 1).

Animosity and frustration clouded Burton's critique of any of Speke's writings, as can be seen in the marginalia of Speke's book *What Led to the Discovery of the Source of the Nile* (BL 1680). Burton's reaction to Speke's account of the attack at Berbera is predictably acrimonious. Speke recalled his capture after the initial attack: "Not knowing a word of that language [Arabic], I spoke in broken Somoli, and heard them say they had not killed any of the English, and would not kill me." Burton wrote in the margin, "could not speak a word" (p. 133). A few pages later, implying cowardice on his companions' part, Speke claimed that Burton and Herne ran away from the tent, and to this Burton simply attached, "a lie" (p. 141).

Later in the narrative, in his account of the Nile expedition, Speke tells the story of his side trip to the north to look for the lake called Ukerewe, which he subsequently named Victoria. Speke summarizes a letter Burton wrote at the time to the Royal Geographical Society in which he said that Speke had volunteered to go north in search of the lake. Next to this paragraph Burton gives us his own reason for letting Speke go— "to get rid of him" (p. 265).

Burton's vociferous "rot" was never more inappropriate, and ironic, than in reponse to Speke's report on the sighting of Lake Victoria. (Burton never went back and altered his annotations; they were evidently spontaneous musings in response to his initial reading.) Three spiteful "rots" appear next to Speke's recollection: "On my inquiring about the lake's length, the man faced to the north, and began nodding his head to it; at the same time he kept throwing forward his right hand, and, making repeated snaps of his fingers, endeavored to indicate something immeasureable; and added that nobody knew, but thought it probably extended to the end of the world" (pp. 311-12). The lake was bigger and more consequential than Burton wished it to be, and Speke's judgment, although flawed, was based on a truth that Burton was unwilling to accept.

There are four books in the Burton Library that particularly intrigue and fascinate me. The first one is entitled *Journals of Major-General Charles G. Gordon* (BL 332). Burton and Gordon shared much in common; their personalities were alike and they had strikingly similar views of the British Empire and British government. As Burton read through Gordon's *Journals,* he discovered that Gordon was absolutely right about many things, and to many passages he appended a "good." As I quote these two statements, you may notice the challenge involved in determining who wrote them—Burton or Gordon. About himself Gordon remarked, "I own to having been very insubordinate to Her Majesty's Government and its officials, but it is my nature, and I cannot help it. I fear I have not even tried to play battledore and shuttlecock with them. I know if I was chief I would never employ *myself*, for I am incorrigible" (p. 59). And about the English Gordon sniped, "We are a wonderful people; it was never our Government which made us a great nation; our Government has been ever the drag on our wheels" (p. 191).

In the second of these books, James Freeman Clarke's *Ten Great Religions,* Burton's irreverence reaches a fever pitch (BL 1244). Isabel Burton admitted that her husband was an agnostic, but the proof of the pudding can be found in Burton's private notes in Clarke's book, in which Clarke postulates that Christianity is an advanced religion and that eventually all humanity will be brought together under its truth. His arguments are countered with blistering attacks and none so short and barbed as that on the title page. Directly under the title "Ten Great Religions" Burton has written "and not one of any good." At the top of chapter ten Burton strikes out against Christianity by declaring, "it does not satisfy humanity. It wants a higher Law, free from its defects." Throughout the text there are comments by Burton that lead one to believe that he thought "race," not religion, was the compelling force in world evolution. In Clarke's book we have caught Burton in one of his most sardonic moods.

Not all books in his library elicited so sober a reaction from Burton, but Burton's responses generally lack humor or playfulness. He took his reading seriously. However, many of Burton's own severe comments today appear outrageous, almost comical. He was not one to mince words or acquiesce to reputation, and this becomes obvious in two of the most interesting books in Burton's library. A page of Jacob Burckhardt's *Arabic Proverbs* is reproduced in Penzer's bibliography to illustrate just how completely Burton had revised the proverbs; in fact, Burton reworked the 782 proverbs almost in their entirety (BL 1532). Burton could not appreciate Burckhardt's obscurity, formality, or blandness, so the editing was done to the Burckhardt style rather than to the Arabic meaning. Quite a few of the proverbs are fairly raunchy, a feature that stimulated rather than deterred Burton. Proverb number thirty-six refers to a silly obstinate fellow who persists in longing for what offends others. Burckhardt's translation is lifeless: "(Yes)—I like my mother-in-law, and I like also that she should make a (disgusting) smell under my nose (crepitum reddendo)." In the margins Burton effortlessly handled the Latin and revived the spirit of the proverb: "I like my mother-in-law, and I like her to fart under my nose."

Burton was a man of extremes and opposites who could move easily from the bawdy to the beautiful. Another literary work in his collection with truly enjoyable annotations is an anthology entitled *A Treasury of English Sonnets,* in which Burton critiques the great sonneteers with astonishing brashness (BL 938). There is little doubt that Burton considered himself a poet; there is also considerable evidence that he knew a great deal about English literature, but when he begins assiduously editing the rhymes of Shakespeare, one can only laugh at his audacity and wonder at his arrogance.

Few men have displayed Burton's brilliance, and few have been so many places or scrutinized with such diligence and energy so many of the world's cultures. There were no geographical or intellectual limits for Burton; his interests knew no bounds. Whether one looks into his life, his writings, or even his library, Burton inevitably opens up new worlds.

The Labyrinthine Paths of Collecting Burton

by Quentin Keynes

I am very delighted to be here today, thanks mainly to Edwards Metcalf. He approached me two or three years ago and said that I must come to this meeting and address you. I was afraid I couldn't, because in the month of October I never come to the United States from England; I show films there at that time. But he was so persuasive that I did come, and I guess I might have come farther than anyone else at this meeting; I flew in from London a couple of days ago.

It is most exciting to be with you all, to know you are interested in a man who is, of course, one of my great heroes, as I believe he is with Edwards Metcalf. I love Americans because you people have done much more about Burton than anybody has in his own country, England. The only Brits who seem to be involved have been John Hayman from Canada, who gave us a very nice talk about Burton, and one or two other people, like Alexander Maitland in London. Perhaps a little bit myself. The most disappointing thing of all was that the Royal Geographical Society never really staged a full celebration of Burton. They did have one speaker, Frank McLynn, who has written a new biography of Burton, published a couple of weeks ago. The only substantive action they have taken in recent years was the refitting of the famous Burton tomb in Mortlake, London, and, if you remember, Don Young mentioned that he and I were the last people to be inside Burton's tomb, and how exciting it was. Don did forget to say one thing: When we got out of the tomb covered with dust, feeling rather extraordinary (just before it was sealed up) there was a little old lady standing outside, who was ninety-seven years old. She said to us, "You know I liked Lady Burton very much because she used to invite me to have tea inside the tomb." She thought that was a very nice thing for Isabel to do for a little girl like her all those years ago, in 1894 or '95. I cannot remember her name, but it was fun to meet someone who had actually known Isabel Burton, within the tomb itself!

I like to collect everything, not only his books and manuscripts, but the people who were interested in him and even knew him. I can tell you I did meet two people, when I was a little boy, who had met Burton. One was Harold Nicolson, the well-known English diplomat and author, who apparently met him when he was about four or five years old. He remembered this fearsome-looking man well, with the big black moustaches, and he was rather worried about how Burton would treat him; in fact, he felt like running away. But Burton was very kind indeed, and took him by the hand and walked him along the corridors of some big building. That's all he could remember. The other man was Colonel Richard Meinertshagen, whom you may have heard of as another incredible adventurer like Burton. He only died comparatively recently. I was sitting next to him at a dinner party in London, and he said, "You know, if you add up the ages of myself and my two sisters it comes to 288." He went on, "I know you are interested in Burton, and I can tell you I met Burton when I was very young, and he was the most extraordinary figure, certainly awe-inspiring, and yet he had a sort of disarming friendliness which made me take to him." That coming from Colonel Meinertzhagen, who was an awe-inspiring figure himself, was, I think, rather wonderful.

Another person who could have known Burton was Lady Nora Barlow, an aunt of mine. She died at the age of 103 in

1989, then the last surviving grandchild of Charles Darwin. I wish I had asked her about Burton; she was old enough to have met him when very young. But Burton did know one of my relatives rather well, as you will learn later.

The collecting of documents and books, however, has been a most exciting thing. I have been a collector of books since a teenager. My father had a world-famous collection of books, and I guess I got into the habit from watching him. So I knew how you collect books; I had the feeling for it. I was very lucky in that regard, but I didn't start with Burton. I started with, of all people, James Joyce. I am still very interested in him, and have a large Joyce collection. I have also collected all sorts of books—books about elephants, books about rhinoceroses, books about Charles Darwin, books about explorers, books about Bugattis. I have odd passions about all kinds of things, but I think of all those passions the greatest one has been for Burton, because Burton was such an enigmatic figure, and many of his books are enigmas. Even his wife, Isabel, was a puzzlement. It has been a sort of James Bond, Sherlock Holmes, Agatha Christie, experience for me to unearth much of the material in my collection.

The first item I am going to tell you about is Burton's "letter book," which is in the first exhibit case. This has been part of a most incredible drama during the last two years. I must explain: for about two months each year I lead expeditions of students to Africa, sometimes with Don Young. Two years ago, while on safari with Don, I suffered an horrendous burglary in the family house in London. It occurred three and a half weeks before my return from Africa, and when I got back to London I was met at the front door by two people, one who lives upstairs and the other below me. Both had long faces, and they said, "We think you have been burgled." And I asked "What do you mean, you think I have been burgled?" And they said, "Well, we haven't, but your place is in a state of complete disarray. We don't know what's been taken." That's normal for me;

my place is always in a state of disarray. It's very much like Burton's own study must have seemed to Isabel. I went upstairs, and I immediately saw that my books were upside down in the most terrible state, and my heart sank. It was one of the most traumatic moments in my life. I will never get over it for as long as I live. Hundreds and hundreds of items had been stolen, including several Burton books. But worst of all, Burton's letter book had gone!

People here have asked me to tell the whole story of the burglary, but I can't possibly do it here, because it takes, literally, over two hours. I was asked to make a ninety-minute video about it. This has been done, and it is being continually updated. The story of the theft is the most extraordinary and dramatic one, straight out of Burton's own life, you might say. I will tell you, however, that a Greek, an Israeli, a Danish girl, and an Englishman were all arrested. The Danish girl was let go because she was considered to be just the girlfriend of the Greek. The Englishman committed suicide; he was the only one who admitted to the burglary. The instigator of this whole thing was an American woman living in London.

There have been Scotland Yard detectives working on it, and I can say that I have gotten back three-quarters of the books. But, unfortunately, I doubt I will ever be able to recover the rest. I had no list of them, and there was no insurance whatsoever on them. I was a very trusting sort of person, which I am not any longer. It has been a disaster in my life—but I must get back to this manuscript.

Sometime in June this year, I was sitting at my desk in London, and I got a call from Sotheby's, from the head of the Manuscripts Department. He said, "Mr. Keynes, we have a very fascinating and important Burton manuscript here in front of us, and we have reason to believe you might be interested in it." I said, "Well, please describe it in detail to me." They did so. I said at once, "I am very interested indeed; I happen to own it." [laughter] They said, "We thought so, because sticking out of this manuscript is a little slip of paper that says, 'The handwriting [on the left-hand page] is definitely that of John Speke, [signed] 'QK.'" They continued, "'QK' is an unusual pair of initials, and we all thought the only person identifiable as 'QK' is Quentin Keynes; therefore, it must be his." And so they called me.

As soon as I told them the manuscript was mine, I was told to zoom down to Sotheby's. Immediately they got their security man in and the police. The police hauled the letter book off to the local police station and rapidly nabbed the man who had mailed it to Sotheby's for auction. The consignor turned out to be an absolute nobody from out of town, and his story was that he worked in a railway lost property office, where objects not claimed after three months are sold to any takers. He said he was the person who put prices on the items, and he had priced my letter book at £5 and had sold it to himself. The police then asked him, "Why did you decide to send it to Sotheby's? What did you know about it?" He answered, "I had heard of a film called *Mountains of the Moon* and I looked at the manuscript, and saw it was about Africa and Burton's name was all over it, so I put two and two together, and thought it must be very valuable not only because it was about Africa but also because Burton's the hero of the film. So I sent it to Sotheby's for sale." He didn't dare come himself to Sotheby's with it.

I then had to write to Edwards Metcalf and say I was sorry, but I probably wouldn't be able to bring the manuscript with me, because it was at the police station. (I had first written to him saying I didn't know where the manuscript was.) Then I besought the police once again to allow me to bring it to the meeting here today, but they said I couldn't, because there was going to be a court case against this man. I said, "That's a real shame—I'm going a long way, thousands of miles, to show this manuscript to people who would passionately like to see it." They replied, "We'll try and get the magistrate to speed the case up." The magistrate agreed to do so, and then—this is a disaster—stated there wasn't enough evidence to convict this man. He was let go. Just as the Greek and Israeli and everyone else accused in this case has been let go! This I find absolutely amazing!

This whole, utterly fantastic story brought in all kinds of extraordinary people, and strange events which are scarcely credible. Similar events seem to have happened to Burton. He had many things stolen from his library during his lifetime, and I sometimes think that some of what I own probably was stolen from him. I don't mean by me, but by people over a hundred years ago [laughter], because I don't see otherwise how they could have come onto the market.

A lot of Burton material came to me in a wonderful and entirely above-board and very English way. One day a man by the name of John Arundell, who is a direct descendant of Lord Arundell (Isabel's cousin) and inherited Wardour Castle in southern England, which belonged to his Lordship Arundell, was wandering around in the castle's attic and saw a large tin box. Inside this tin box he found some old papers and quite a few old books. He examined them and saw the names "Richard Burton" and "Isabel Burton" time and time again. Who were they? He wasn't quite sure who they were. Luckily a friend knew and said to him, "You better not chuck those things out, because Richard Burton's quite a famous person and so is Isabel, his wife." It appeared that Isabel had left this box and its contents, unbeknownst to anybody (she never published this fact anywhere), to Lord Arundell of Wardour. It had been sitting around without the contents having been looked at by anybody until Anthony Hobson of Sotheby's saw them.

At the time the box came to Sotheby's attention I was sweltering in the jungles of Belize in Central America. I didn't know anything about its discovery, until suddenly Hobson cabled me in Belize suggesting that I shoot some bids to him in London. He'd only sent very sparse details, but I told him which items I wanted the most. I said, "I don't have any money, I am in the jungles of Belize, and I am sweating hot, and I don't know what to do. Please help me." Anthony Hobson is an absolutely wonderful person, and a great friend of mine and of my father's; we had known him for years. He managed to get all the material most wanted by me in the Wardour Castle sale. Mr. Metcalf was competing against me in the auction—we didn't even know each other then! Hobson said, "You shouldn't use your own name when you buy lots in this sale, you must be very secretive and use "phony" names. He selected the most unusual names for me—Mr. Postlethwaite, Mr. Pottinger, etc. Nobody had the faintest idea who these people were. If anything they thought they were probably new Burton collectors. The truth has all come out long since. I am both Mr. Postlethwaite and Mr. Pottinger!

The contents of the box proved to be the most mouth-watering material. I was sitting in London just a few days ago thinking about what I should bring along to San Marino. I picked all the bits and pieces you can view in the glass cases. There is so much I wanted to bring, but these items seemed to me some of the most fascinating of all—most of them quite unknown to the world at large.

The letter book itself consists of copies of letters Burton wrote from Africa between 1854 and 1859. He copied them quite nicely and they're easy to read. There are also letters to him and detailed bills that he received in East Africa for supplies, etc. So you can see what he spent on various things during this period in Africa.

It contains an exact description of the attack by the Somalis in Berbera, written not only by Burton but by Speke and Lieutenant Herne; all three riveting accounts are in Burton's hand. I've never had time to compare the autograph texts with the printed versions as published in *First Footsteps* in 1856, but they do describe one of the most dramatic events in the lives of both Burton and Speke and the one commemorated brilliantly in the famous portrait of Burton by Sir Frederic Leighton that you all know. The Leighton painting is on the dust wrappers of almost every Burton biography published in recent years. I refer, of course, to the scar depicted on Burton's cheek, which was the result of a Somali spear thrown at him.

Apart from those three accounts there is also a delightful touch. On the last page is a list of Burton's close friends and their addresses—this was his address book, as it were. As you look down the list you see all these eminent people's names and suddenly, in the middle, there is "Isabel Arundell," followed by her address, listed as if she was just anybody. Of course, Isabel became Richard's wife only in 1861. I thought it was very typical that she wouldn't be at the top—just in the middle somewhere. [laughter]

There is another touch where Isabel is involved. At one point you come to the middle of the book, and there you'll notice about twenty pages have been excised, although there are stubs left still revealing the first two words of each line. You can see that they've been cut out with a knife, not a pair of scissors. What on earth was this about? Why did she cut out these particular pages? Nothing else is excised from the volume. That is one of the more enigmatic puzzles of the letter book. It has come apart at the spine even more than when I first owned it. Since the burglars roughed it up, I don't know how many hands have held it unkindly.

The man that was arrested was not the original burglar who admitted the theft of my books. I will tell you why I think he happened upon the journal. It is the only actual manuscript in my whole collection, as far as I know, that was taken. I'd had a beautiful cloth box made for it. It was on a shelf along with five other very special African books all in similar boxes, and he must have pulled all six of these boxes off together. When he found the letter book wasn't a printed book, I think he took it to that "lost property office" to get rid of it. That's my theory. The man from the lost property office may be telling a little bit of the truth, but not all of it.

All the books that were next to it in the other boxes were

quite extraordinary. The first was John Speke's own copy of his famous book *What Led to the Discovery of the Source of the Nile*, corrected all the way through by him with new information he wanted to add for a future edition. The volume was signed at the beginning with his name and his address. And inside was a letter from Speke to one of the printers, telling him off for not noticing some mistakes and that kind of thing.

I had in that same group the most dramatic copy in existence of Stanley's famous book *How I Found Livingstone*. In the front was a piece of paper stuck in by the person who received the book—Agnes Livingstone, Livingstone's oldest daughter. That was the closest person Stanley could give the book to, since Livingstone was dying at that point, in Africa. I love this inscription. It says, "To Miss Agnes Livingstone, the daughter of the great traveller who I met at Ujiji on August 10, 1872, . . . Henry M. Stanley." He meant 1871. I thought "who I met at Ujiji" sounded as if he had been at a cocktail party where he had chanced to meet Dr. Livingstone! Yet, it was one of the most dramatic meetings in history.

I have to add here one little footnote. I knew the explorer's grandson, Dick Stanley, who recently died. I was staying with him and his father, Major Denzel Stanley, one weekend when I asked Major Stanley, "Do you think your father really said 'Dr. Livingstone, I presume.'" He got quite huffy, as only an English major can, and said, "What else could he have said in the circumstances?" [laughter] When you think about it, what else could he have said? We might say that even today. Anyway, poor Stanley's question has been treated as a standard joke for over a hundred years now.

The third dramatic volume was a copy of Livingstone's first book, *Missionary Travels*. It was dedicated in print to Sir Roderick Murchison, who was president of the Royal Geographical Society at the time. But this was the actual copy he gave Sir Roderick, which contained a long inscription to him in his huge handwriting. Another of the boxed books stolen together was the only known proof copy of *How I Found Livingstone*. An 1872 proof must be one of the earliest publisher's proofs, for one doesn't think of publishers as preparing proofs in those days. It's slightly different from the published version. The last book was quite incredible—Robert Moffat's book *Missionary Labors* of 1842. Moffat was, of course, Livingstone's father-in-law. It is a copy inscribed by him to a fellow missionary. He wrote a flowery religious inscription, and then he signed it, along with his wife, his daughter Mary, who married Livingstone, and all the other children in the family, as well as an African girl that the missionaries had found and brought up. And, amazingly, at the bottom of the page were the signatures of David Livingstone and Henry M. Stanley. This is the only piece of paper in the world, I believe, that is signed by both Livingstone and Stanley together.

You may ask how it could have been signed by Livingstone and Stanley as well as the others. Obviously, the missionary had asked that the book be inscribed to him, and he then much later heard that Livingstone was giving a lecture somewhere and took it over to him and had him sign it. Later, news came that Stanley was giving a lecture, and the missionary asked him for a signature too. But I am getting rather sidetracked. I only meant to explain why the letter book was taken. Luckily, I got all those five unique, signed books back together via the police. Over four hundred books were returned by the police to me in various states of repair, but the letter book has not suffered too badly—only the back is torn rather worse than before.

Other things on display are noteworthy. The blue paper-bound pamphlet in the first case is the patent for a revolver that Burton designed to shoot from horseback. Very useful if you are in a hurry to kill someone from a horse. He thought it might be useful for soldiers. I have never heard of another copy, and I don't think there is a copy in Burton's own collection. This volume must have come from Burton's library. How else could it now be with me? I don't know.

Then there is an extraordinary manuscript excerpt of a letter from John Speke to his mother. It was found by my cousin Felix Pryor, who is one of the most brilliant analysts of autograph material in the world. He was looking through some documents, and saw this odd bit of paper sticking out of a book, and as soon as he noticed "Your loving son, J. H. Speke," he realized it was a little bit of a letter to his mother. On each side there is an amazing statement. One says in summary that "B" (Burton) never really went to Mecca and Medina, and Harar in the normal sense—he was taken there by Africans, and they got him up to all kinds of tricks. Exactly what that's all about, I don't know. It's rather ambiguous and strange. On the other side he says, "I am sorry to be writing to you about such a rotten person"—in other words, he means, Burton. It is a very nasty thing to say, but I am glad I have it, because it shows up Speke's character a little bit, although I don't want to be unfair to Speke, as I will explain later in the talk.

As you know, "The Scented Garden" was the last work that Burton retranslated, and he just had a half page to go when he died in October 1890. This was one of the most sensational things that Isabel burnt, after his death, although the firing of his diaries was a far more destructive act. It has to be said, however, that the destruction of this manuscript caused much more comment in the newspapers. Nobody had ever known exactly how many pages were destroyed. All anyone knew was that it was a painstakingly accurate translation from the Arabic of the erotic "Scented Garden." Its forthcoming publication had actually been announced in a printed notice giving the title and date when it would be coming out. After Isabel burnt the manuscript, she heard that someone was claiming that they had another copy, and would publish it. So she composed this extraordinary document, which can be seen under the glass, about how she would "get" anybody who tried to claim they owned the manuscript. There is a little envelope which says on the outside, "This will trap them," which I love.

These documents have never been seen since they were put in the Arundell tin box. The whole case on the far right is about "The Scented Garden," and it includes a copy of Isabel's long explanation in the *Morning Post* of London as to why she burnt the manuscripts. That illustrates high drama, as do many of the other papers exhibited.

Another item is a subscription proposed for a monument to John Speke. It gives all the names of the people who subscribed. Sir Roderick Murchison gave £20, Captain Grant gave £10, and Burton gave £5. The document gives us an indication about how Burton felt about Speke. There is another rather obscure little pamphlet published by Speke's sister about this monument, which was put up on the north side of Hyde Park in London.

The rarest book of Burton's, as everyone knows, is *A Complete System of Bayonet Exercise*. It is one that none of us collectors can find. I have actually had five copies in my hands at one time or another, but they must be just about the only known copies in the world. Each one is slightly different; each is held by a major library. The one at the Huntington is Burton's own copy. I thought it would be interesting to find a contemporary review of this rare book, and I acquired the one on display, published the same year as the book. The reviewer doesn't treat the exercise as very helpful training for the army!

On display also is the actual contract between Burton and the printer of his *Arabian Nights*, Philip Waterlow, from the famous firm of Waterlow & Sons. This is signed by Isabel and Richard Burton. Isabel didn't like Burton's translation of *The Arabian Nights*, because it had so many naughty things in it, so she excised 203 pages' worth of such text. Burton was amused, and annoyed, by this, so he decided, "Well, damn it! I'm going to collect all those 203 naughty pages and publish another book called 'The Black Book of the Arabian Nights.'" It was to contain only the naughty pages. The preface was as far as he got. What I have is that original unpublished, unknown, preface.

The Labyrinthine Paths of Collecting Burton

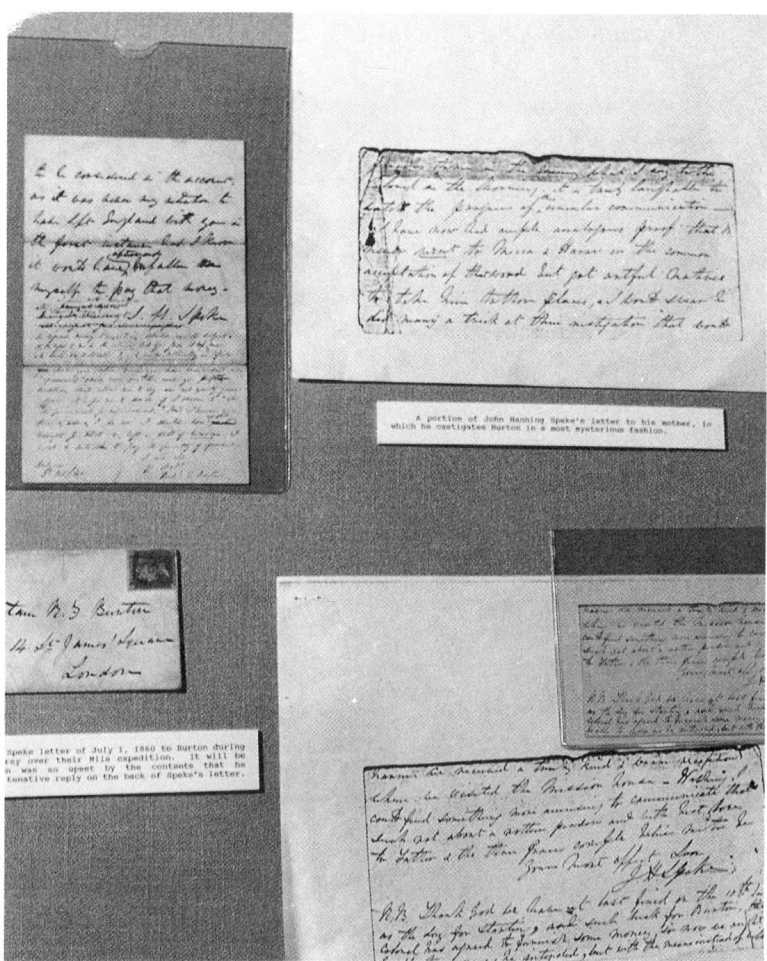

On exhibition at the Burton conference were documents from the collection of Quentin Keynes, including letters of John Hanning Speke, one to his mother complaining about how "rotten" Burton was. Photo courtesy of Earl Beadle.

That's another amusing little bit of a textual tiff between husband and wife.

I have never known a husband and wife to publish different accounts of their trips taken together. Both Isabel and Richard wrote descriptions, and completely separate versions, of the Passion Play at Oberammergau. Similarly, in Richard's book on Brazil, she wrote in the preface how she really didn't agree with a lot of the book, but she was publishing it anyway. [laughter]

Where has the correspondence between Richard and Isabel gone? There obviously was a lot because he was always telling her what to do: "Pay, pack and follow." I have managed to find three bits of correspondence: two are from Isabel to Richard and one from Richard to Isabel. Richard's letter to Isabel is a series of notes asking her to do this and that, to pay this and that, and to see so and so. Isabel's letters talk about her own daily activities. They are very loving letters. Burton's letter starts off, "My Darling." Isabel's ends in one with the most extraordinary signature, "KTT" in big letters and in the other with "Puss." What "KTT" means I don't know. If anyone can help me, I would appreciate it. Other letters may exist; Edwards Metcalf told me he might possibly have one or two.

I recently discovered the only description of Speke's and Burton's expeditions in East Africa by an African, written in his own language. It was published in an obscure magazine, the *Uganda Journal*, in 1934, and translated into English by the Englishman who interviewed the old man, Om. Ham Mukasa, who told the story. This old man could not read, so he could not refer to Speke's or Burton's own books. He gives a genuine African account of something that happened eighty years before. It is very intriguing to read.

Next is one of my favorite documents—a dramatic letter from Speke to Burton written when they were having their controversy over the source of the Nile. It starts off, "Dear Sir." They had known each other on two expeditions, by their first names presumably, but now they are down to "Dear Sir." The first sentence states, "Since you are <u>desirous</u> of shunning me. . . ." Burton was very upset, obviously, by this letter, and was in such a rage that on the back he wrote his reply, and it begins, "Dear Sir, I am <u>not</u> desirous of shunning you. . . ." I don't think you could find a more dramatic letter, between the two leading adversaries in the Nile controversy. I have six or seven or eight other letters from Speke to Burton.

A most enigmatic item is the blue piece of paper on which James Grant, who went on the Nile expedition with Captain Speke, wrote that Speke would not be coming to the British Association meeting. That presumably was the Bath meeting, which Speke did finally agree to attend, but he killed himself before the debate. The strange thing is that it is written a year before the meeting took place. The note doesn't have a greeting, and has no full date, but is written in Grant's large hand.

Fawn Brodie loved the next item, and she wrote a whole chapter on it after I showed it to her. There has always been a controversy as to how Burton translated *The Arabian Nights*. What version did he use? He obviously had an Arabic original, but did he consult English translations? The man he admired for his translation, and the man who admired him, was John Payne. Payne had done an edition of *The Arabian Nights* in nine volumes. (It is not so well known today and rather hard to find.) Volume nine he dedicated to Sir Richard Burton, with a great deal of thanks. As Fawn Brodie shows in the appendix to her biography, Burton simply took a copy of Payne's book and tore it apart. He laid the printed pages on the table in front of him, with the Arabic original alongside. He wrote his own version above Payne's text, and changed everything he didn't approve of in Payne's translation. I have brought over several samples of Burton's revisions to show how it was done; in London I have twenty or thirty more pages. It is a very important historical document because it proves a point so definitely.

A piece that I had never seen, and I only got in London just before I left last week, is an extract, printed in twenty copies, of

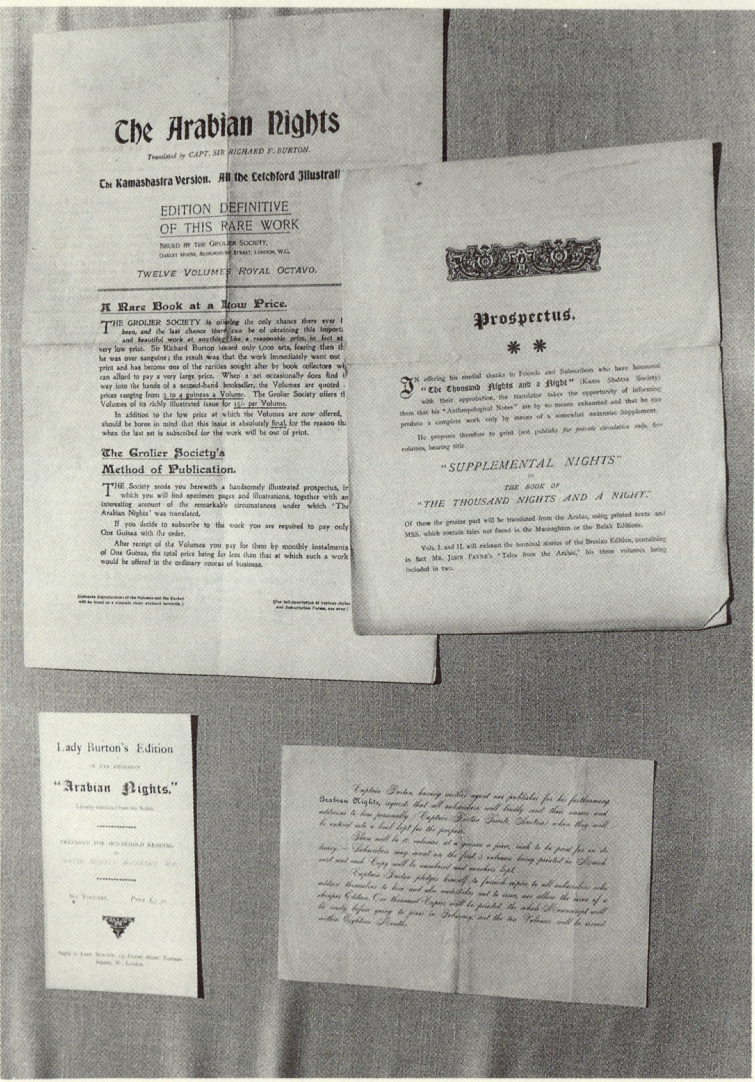

Announcements of various editions of *The Arabian Nights*, from the collection of Quentin Keynes, including "Lady Burton's Edition." Photo courtesy of Earl Beadle.

part of volume nine of Payne's translation dedicated to Burton. It is inscribed, oddly enough, by John Payne to the English writer Matthew Arnold. I thought this a very exciting thing to find, so suddenly.

There are also the various announcements of Burton's Kama Shastra publications from Benares, which, of course, is an invented place of publication. One, with italic letters, says that if you want to get a copy of *The Arabian Nights* you must apply to Captain Burton personally, and he will attend to it. I think that's a rather nice touch.

One amusing item is Isabel Burton's pamphlet, printed at her own expense, and intended for high British government officials, to persuade them that Burton should be knighted. She says that's what he wants most of all, but actually it was what Isabel wanted! It is a rather sly bit of paper, but quite important. She says all the wonderful things about Richard you would expect her to say. If you read the top, you will see that nobody is meant to see this—it's private and secret, and only ministers are allowed to have copies. She was always doing that sort of thing. That is why I feel ambivalent about her. In some ways she was a dreadful woman, and in others she was a brave woman. She really was devoted to Richard. She would do anything for him. This is proved in every document I have ever seen, and everything that has been written about her. It is very hard to fathom—but perhaps it isn't—why she burnt Burton's manuscripts at the end of his life. She was an ardent Catholic. Of course, the cemetery at Mortlake where Richard Burton is buried is Catholic. The way she said, in her *Life of Burton*, that he got to be a Catholic, and therefore could be buried there, is dramatic. As soon as he died she rushed out into the street and got an Italian priest, and she said, "My husband is very ill, will you please come and give him the last rites." I think the cleric must have looked at the body rather strangely. Anyway, he administered the rites and that satisfied her. He was now a Catholic and could be buried in Mortlake

Cemetery. Of course, Isabel was later buried next to him.

Another item I have is a Catholic Bible printed in red and black, with clasps. It was inscribed by Isabel to Burton. I don't think it has been opened since.

So these pieces are more or less what I brought to show you, but there are some other points I want to bring up. I should apologize for the fact that I am the only person speaking at this conference who is not a scholar in any sense. I never even finished what you would call high school. At the age of sixteen I told my parents that I wasn't going back to my elite boarding school. I wanted to start exploring. I stood on the roof of our house all night, I remember, and refused to come back in. They gave up trying to make me go back, and I then went to live in France and Switzerland, like Burton. They say that people who own pets long enough come to look like their animals. Well, I think I have come to resemble Burton in some ridiculous way by the life I've lived. [laughter]

The Foreign Office in England asked about my profession, but I have never really been certain what my profession is. They said, "What do you do?" and I told them, "I go all over the place." "Oh, you're an explorer then," and they put "Profession: Explorer" in my passport. I don't think it's fair to Burton's memory to be called an explorer, because he really was one—I am a sham one. My life is spent going to remote places and making films of what I see. In that sense I am perhaps an explorer, but mainly an explorer of people and of animals and of objects, more than an explorer of great tracts of land.

I have mentioned that there are many enigmas involved in the Burton things one obtains. There are often strange inscriptions in his books. I try to get as many as I can inscribed from Burton to other people. It was hard for him to give away many books, because he wasn't usually in the right place at the right time. For instance, one of the rarest and most delightful Burton publications is *A New System of Sword Exercise for Infantry*, a slim little red volume. There are two issues of it, one with two swords crossed on the cover and one without them. One copy I discovered had an inscription in Burton's distinctive hand on the flyleaf, "A mon ami Constantine." Constantine was the man who taught Burton fencing, so it's probably the best copy of that book one could ever find. I was excited to get it.

Another object I came across that was very exciting was an early version of the portrait of Burton by Sir Frederic Leighton. It is very similar to the famous one I mentioned earlier that's in the National Portrait Gallery in London, with the scar on his cheek. I've studied it for a long time, and in some ways it is just as good as the final portrait. It is a lovely painting to have; it is the greatest picture of Burton ever made.

I have told you about "collecting people," and how I always admired Burton, and how I would like to be related to him. I am related to a lot of interesting people, I am lucky to be able to say, but not to Burton. I never could find any connection. One day, however, I met Peter Speke, a delightful person, who is the nearest living relative to John Speke. He lives in a fine, fourteenth-century mini-castle in Somerset on the estate of John Speke. Speke's place was called Jordans and Peter's place is called Rowlands, but they're actually on the same estate. While Peter and I were sitting at the immense ancient oak table in his stone dining room having lunch, I was looking at this wonderful stained-glass window, with coats of arms all over it. I suddenly noticed my own family's coat of arms—the blue Keynes coat of arms. I said, "Peter, why on earth have you got my family's coat of arms in your house? That isn't fair. What's the story?" He said, "Just a minute."

So after lunch we went down to a little twelfth-century church in Dowlish Wake, a village near his farm. On the left-hand side of the altar was a splendid tomb of a knight lying with his toes turned up, his arms folded, and his sword beside him. Peter said, "Come around and look at this." On the side of the tomb was inscribed, "John Speke, thirteen hundred something to fourteen hundred something." On the other side of his body lay his wife. Incised on that same side were similar dates with the name Joan Keynes. So there Peter Speke and I were standing, related to both husband and wife with the same names, 490 years later. So it turned out I was related to the wrong side, since I was always more of a Burton fan than a Speke fan. [laughter and clapping] But I can't help it—I'll have to live and bear it. It's a matter of history! Thank you.

Discussion

Question: Do you think that Isabel kept more things than were found in the box you talked about? Do you think she might have held back other things?

Keynes: No. I really think that was everything. I haven't heard of anything else, and it is unlikely. She had two assistants who were helping her burn Burton's journals. She must have been more attached to her cousin Lord Arundell than to anybody else.

Question: As a longtime Burton collector, can you tell us about Penzer's collection of Burton?

Keynes: As you know, Mr. Penzer's house was blitzed in 1939 at the very beginning of the war. The only remaining Burton diary was destroyed at that time. This had come into his possession because it was saved by Minnie Plowman, who was working with Isabel's sister. I think because I have hardly found anything of Penzer's anywhere that most of his collection must also have been burned in the blitz. His own copy of his bibliography was sold at auction a few years ago, and unfortunately I was on an expedition in Borneo and I couldn't bid on it, or I would have it now. I don't know who has it. That is one of the few things of Penzer's that I've heard about. I've seen a couple of letters from him and that's all.

Question: You mentioned there was a statue of Speke in Hyde Park. Is there one of Burton anywhere in Britain?

Keynes: Not that I know of. I'm afraid the only monument is the Mortlake tomb. There is a small plaque in Bagamoyo, Tanzania, which is where Speke and Burton set off from to go west. That is nothing much. It is a shame—there really should be one.

Question: Do you think the Burton material held by private collectors today would alter our perception of Burton in a significant way?

Keynes: I can think of nothing that I have come across that would. Between Edwards Metcalf and myself, and a couple of others like Burke Casari, that covers the number of collectors. I could be wrong. I'm always finding things.

Question: You mentioned a patent for a pistol. Was there ever a model made of it?

Keynes: No, it was never actually manufactured, but the details are in the pamphlet.

Don Young's comments from the audience: The original pistol is in the Orleans House Library, Richmond-upon-Thames, and it's on public display. This is where Isabel deposited material after Burton's death. It is an Italian-made flintlock, heavy saddle pistol with a swivel hand mount—probably an Italian carbine that he modified into a pistol by sawing it down and putting a handle on it, so a person on horseback could easily use it.

Question: Did you recover any of the documents that you said were stolen?

Keynes: As I think I said, I did recover three-quarters of them. Unfortunately, the quarter left includes some terrific things. Heartbreaking.

Question: Are items from that missing quarter likely to show up from time to time?

Keynes: I don't think so. The whole trouble was that the main thief committed suicide. He was going to tell the court where the material was. He never did tell his lawyer before he killed himself. It was a huge case; he was up on £100,000 bail. He was a brilliant man whom lots of people knew, but he was berserk in the head. He never got any money out of it, as far as I know. Many of the ones taken were beautiful color-plate books, some of African animals. I'm afraid the books have all been cut up.

Question: You mentioned the hour-and-a-half TV interview.

Keynes: Yes, but I wouldn't allow it to be shown on TV because it's too libelous. I talked about a lot of things that I and the police are supposing. It's private. I just had to make it because one has to make some kind of record. It's so complicated. I show it only to my friends. It is apparently very interesting to people. They watch it on the edge of their seats.

Question: Are there any plans to edit and publish the Burton letter book?

Keynes: I am thinking about it now that I have it back. Remember that I haven't had it for two years. It's getting rather tattered. I want to do something about it. It's so intriguing.

Question: Have you been able to accumulate any material from Burton's career in India?

Keynes: I haven't got the Karachi brothel report. [laughter] There is very little extant, as far as I know, of his time in India.

Question: I am curious because there should have been something on paper if he was in a staff position.

Keynes: I know there has been very little found from those years. I forgot to describe probably the earliest known Burton manuscript surviving, which I brought. It is a satirical account of life in the Anglo-Indian army in the 1840s and a glossary of expressions soldiers use. That I do want to publish, and it should be very amusing. It is difficult to decipher. I think we can do it. The paper is watermarked 1843, but there is a postmark on a letter addressed to him as ensign in 1846, so I estimate it must have been done around 1845-46. He just used this letter as a piece of scrap paper. That really is the only Indian material I know of.

James Casada's comment from the audience: Because the official records are fairly complete, I have some doubts personally about whether the Karachi report was ever actually written. Fawn Brodie goes on at great length about what might have happened to the document. I think it's possible it was never written at all.

Keynes: I agree with you. He loved to boast about shocking things that he did. He was supposed to have killed someone, but, of course, he didn't.

Question: Is there any evidence whether or not Burton dabbled in codes, because it would seem to be a very logical thing for him to be interested in?

Keynes: I don't personally think so.

Don Young from the audience: When you can write twenty-nine languages you don't need codes. [laughter]

Question: Do you know of any Burton manuscript material dealing with mesmerism and the occult?

Keynes: There were some sold by Sotheby's last month. That's all I know about.

Alan Jutzi's comment from the audience: There are at least a half-dozen books in his library that deal with those topics. There is also a book on Blavatsky in which he debunks a lot of the things she espouses. He was involved with mesmerism and the occult in the '70s and '80s and actually did attend spiritualism meetings. He gave a lecture one time to a spiritualist group essentially debunking it.

Keynes: I have a book in my collection with notes and minutes about Burton's speech.

Question: When Burton was knighted, were there any special or interesting things about his knighthood that were made public?

Keynes: I really don't know much about that.

Don Young's comment from the audience: There is a wonderful story you may know. When the notice of his knighthood came with a pile of other letters it was addressed to "Sir Richard Burton, KCMG." He tossed it over to Isabel and said, "Send this back, it must be addressed to someone else," knowing exactly how she felt about his knighthood. She opened it and it was the announcement.

Comment from the audience: I think it's worth mentioning Burton's family motto in Latin as translated was "Honor not honors," and I think everything we've heard in this two-day seminar supports the fact that he lived true to that creed.

Keynes: One thing I've just thought of pertains to films about Richard Burton. For years I've wanted to have a major film made about his life. Fawn Brodie sold the rights of her biography to Paul Radin, who made *Born Free,* about a lion. John Hopkins wrote a script and John Frankenheimer was going to direct, and I went and had a conference with them in California. They couldn't find enough money to get it going. Then Sidney Lumet wanted to make it. That fell through. Of course, *Mountains of the Moon* was released—it was based on a book that the author called "faction." It's fiction, not a true story.

There are rather a lot of mistakes in that book. I had a letter from Sir Richard Attenborough, Sir David Attenborough's brother, an actor and also director who made the great film *Gandhi*. He is very interested in making a film biography of Burton. I tried to get David Lean to do it, who is the obvious choice since he directed *Lawrence of Arabia*. But David Lean is a very old man now, and his wife (who was in the middle of reading *Vikram and the Vampire*, the Indian stories translated by Burton, when I spoke to her) told me that David Lean would never do a film unless he thought of it first himself. He doesn't like to have suggestions from other people. I am just hoping that Richard Attenborough can put together the film from the right sources. You can make several films, I think you all agree, about his life. A really good one directed by someone from the classical school of film would be a wonderful thing.

Concluding Remarks

by Jim Casada

I want to look at four basic areas in the study of Burton: the history of Burton bibliography, the collecting of Burton material, the research opportunities that still remain open to Burton scholars, and finally, projects that require immediate attention.

For anyone who is, or has considered becoming, a Burton aficionado, the proper starting point is Norman Penzer's massive bibliography. A true labor of love, this book was published in 1923 although Penzer likely had aimed for 1921, the centenary of Burton's birth. The book was originally published in only five hundred copies, and for a collector to own one of these is to hold a prize. It has since been reprinted twice, once in London and once in this country, and the reprints are available on the out-of-print market if one does a bit of digging.

Penzer's bibliography is extraordinarily accurate, although not perfect. No bibliography is; the best one can hope for is comprehensiveness. Burke Casari has already indicated all too clearly how much I personally have erred, and we will shortly address areas that all of us have thus far overlooked. For the time in which he wrote and for the existing state of of bibliographical technique and knowledge, though, Penzer did a truly outstanding job. He was remarkably thorough; I found perhaps three or four dozen printed items that he omitted, Burke Casari has added several more, and doubtless there are others still to come.

If there is a single major weakness in Penzer's work, it is that he identified too closely with Burton and liked him too much. All of us who study Burton to some degree share that weakness. This is not to suggest that Penzer's approach was hagiographical, for that would be simplistic. Yet he was not quite as far removed historically from Burton as we are, and that was a liability.

My own book, *Sir Richard F. Burton: A Biobibliographical Study*, was undertaken primarily with an eye to updating Penzer's but also in order to touch on one or two areas which he did not cover. A "biobibliography" employs a combination of bibliographical and biographical techniques, an approach I have used previously in studies of other Africanists—Sir Henry Morton Stanley, Sir Harry H. Johnston, and Dr. David Livingstone.

I undertook another task, which in fact Penzer could have performed had he so chosen: assembling a reasonably comprehensive list of extant manuscript holdings relating to Burton. Those in both public institutions and private collections are covered (the two most important private collections in the world are of course represented in this room in the persons of Quentin Keynes and Edwards Metcalf). There are other noteworthy collections, including Burke Casari's, and doubtless further papers in private hands remain undiscovered—an area which needs greater study, as I will suggest in more detail below.

Penzer is also a good guide to the second area I want to address, that of collecting Burton material. Quentin Keynes has given us a marvelous anecdotal overview of what he has done as a Burton collector. His efforts and those of Edwards Metcalf simply cannot be repeated, but those of you who are or wish to become Burton collectors have a challenge before you—printed material. Burton wrote prolifically, and his books are still regularly available on the out-of-print market.

What I want to do at present is simply to suggest some directions that collecting of original works by Burton might take. You can approach Burton as the author of original works. There are literally dozens of books in this area alone, and in many cases there are various editions, both from his time and in modern reprinted form. I learned here at this conference that Dane Kennedy has edited a reprint, with a new introduction, of *Goa, and the Blue Mountains* (recently published by the University of California Press). It is a real challenge to obtain the originals of Burton's works; you will discover that in many instances there are different editions, variants, and the like. I don't want to say a great deal about price, although Penzer included much of this sort of information. You will pay dearly for first editions. A book is worth, ultimately, what someone is willing to pay for it. As a rule, Burton material will not come cheap, but there are always treasures that have gone unnoticed for years to be found in a general bookseller's store. Such discoveries bring a sense of rare pleasure.

Another approach is to focus on Burton as a translator. There are numerous editions of *The Arabian Nights* alone—some excellent, some indifferent. Penzer was quite critical of pirated editions and of the various "clubs" that issued *Arabian Nights*, but I disagree with him here. What he forgot was that these editions made more opportunities for those of us who are collectors, and if he were alive today he might feel differently about it. There have been scores of twentieth-century selections printed from Burton's translated works, often by clubs specializing in limited editions. Many of these are numbered copies printed on fine paper or featuring fine bindings. These in themselves represent an interesting collecting challenge.

Perhaps the biggest challenge of all would be to attempt to form an extensive holding of Burton's shorter printed material as it appeared in articles, reviews, notes, published letters, and the like. This would be a major undertaking, though the monetary expense would not be nearly as important as the expenditure of time. Burton's works deserve better than the fate of being leather-bound prisoners in glass-fronted cages. They are made to be read and reread, to be consulted, and to be studied.

You never come to one of Burton's major works, even a second time, without learning something new. The footnotes alone, as Burke Casari has suggested, can be a joyous study. To be sure, we can admire some of his books for their visual impact, because many of them were beautifully produced, but they are far too little used from an intellectual perspective. Burton's biographers have frequently failed to utilize Burton himself, the ultimate source, in studying the man. In fact, most of his recent biographers have not read Burton's own works as they should, from the point of view of their content, and perhaps a few thoughts on the major biographies are in order.

Let us begin with Byron Farwell, an American who has published a number of books on the Victorian era. Farwell's *Burton* has a twofold strength: it offers both a generally balanced and convincing portrait of Burton and a thorough and accurate treatment of the available printed sources. His work is second in merit only to Fawn Brodie's *The Devil Drives*, the best life of Burton done to date. Like virtually everything she wrote, *The Devil Drives* uses psychoanalytic techniques to delve into its subject, a method that can certainly be questioned. It is difficult enough to rely on the results of psychoanalysis in writing about a live person, yet Burton has been subjected to repeated post-mortems with less than ample information and no opportunity to respond. With that caveat understood, the fact remains that Brodie researched widely and well. She asked many of the right questions of her material, she wrote well, and she knew how to sell books; the title *The Devil Drives* is a bookseller's dream.

Brodie remains the point of departure for future biographical efforts, partly because other recent works have been disappointing or less complete in their approach. Michael Hastings' study, *Sir Richard Burton: A Biography*, was an outgrowth of the fine British Broadcasting Corporation production on the search for the Nile sources. Because it touches on information that no one else has unearthed, it should be required reading for serious students of Burton, but it is quite weak at some points.

Glenn S. Burne's volume in the Twayne English Authors series looks at Burton as a man of letters; in certain areas (particularly a chapter on "Exotic Erotica") it is especially valuable. William Harrison's *Burton and Speke* has been described as "faction," and it purports to mix fact with fiction. Actually, much adherence to the former is difficult to discern. The book made money and provided the material for the movie *Mountains of the Moon*, but it adds nothing to our understanding of either Burton or Speke or of the relationship between the two. Finally there is Edward Rice's recently published life, *Captain Sir Richard Francis Burton*, produced, surprisingly, without the consultation of anyone in this room. The book was apparently written in a secluded study, with the assistance of interlibrary loan. There are literally hundreds of unattributed quotations, many of them unknown to me despite two and a half decades spent examining a great deal of Burton material. Then, too, Rice devotes some two hundred pages to a metaphysical exercise on Sufism, which is at best tangentially related to Burton's Indian career. Best-seller status notwithstanding, the book is a striking disappointment.

This brief overview of modern biographies suggests that much remains to be done. As I have said in the biographical portion of my own study, however, I suspect that a definitive life will never be written. That is just as well because those of us who are in the Burton "industry" would be sorely disappointed if we had nothing more about which to speculate. As Alan Jutzi said in the conclusion to his presentation: "Burton inevitably opens up new worlds." As one lovingly returns to him time after time, it is always to discover new perspectives. We are fortunate that such is the case.

With that in mind, I would like to add some thoughts on other prospects for research. Certainly Lady Burton needs careful work. There is no decent biography of her. Albertine Gaur of the British Library is presumably still working on what promises to be a fine life of Lady Burton. We also need more reprints of Burton's better works. While he was very uneven as a writer, some of his more serious travel works need to be reprinted, with substantial introductions that evaluate these works both in their original contexts and from the standpoint of how well they have weathered the test of time. The edition of *Goa* that Dane Kennedy prepared is just such a project. Burke Casari has discovered information that all of us have missed; one wishes the British Library's newspaper collection at Colindale could somehow be transferred to Lincoln, Nebraska! Certainly there is ample scope for work in newspapers. Burton's letters-to-the-editor must surely have appeared in dozens of newspapers, and they can be found only through painstaking work. Palmer's *Index to the Times* is but a starting point; regional and provincial newspapers must be a veritable gold mine of information.

We also need to turn known manuscripts to better advantage, especially those that have been largely overlooked. Material at the Royal Asiatic Society offers a good example, but even the supposedly well-used documents at the Royal Geographical Society have not yielded the fruit that they promise. There are no doubt manuscripts still to be unearthed. It would be helpful to form a list of somewhere between fifty and one hundred of Burton's intimates, his circle of friends, and to trace their papers. It seems plausible that Burton letters would have ended up in such hands. Isabel did not have a chance to burn Burton's letters, at least, for most of them would have been in the hands of correspondents. A concerted effort to trace such material would be quite useful, and Quentin Keynes mentioned a list that might well be a starting point for such a project.

Official documents relevant to Burton's military and consular careers may still be unearthed at the India Office (although it is quite likely that the heralded Karachi report never existed). There should be additional manuscripts awaiting discovery at the Public Record Office. Burton's treatment of sexual matters has been a preoccupation of modern biographers, yet they offer much more speculation than fact. Possibly in this case, as well as in some of the unidentified or unsigned articles Burke Casari mentioned, textual analysis, aided by computer, may prove to be of help. Then we turn to the ultimate challenge, Burton as a linguist. Few are likely to have the mastery of languages that Burton cultivated, but here lies unplowed ground for someone. Similarly, we need more work on those contemporaries who were involved in Burton's work. Several examples come immediately to mind. Alex Maitland wrote an interesting biography of John Speke, but without consulting various materials which have since come to light, particularly the extensive collection of the papers of James Augustus Grant, Speke's companion on the latter's second journey to the sources of the Nile. Grant's papers, now housed at the National Library of Scotland, include hundreds of letters as well as a diary covering not only the African years but the subsequent period through 1876. The diary runs to well over a thousand closely written pages, and it incorporates many references to Burton.

The papers of Verney Lovett Cameron are available on microfilm, also at the National Library of Scotland. Cameron went with Burton to the Gold Coast, an adventure Burton undertook in the latter part of his career as one of many attempts to make his fortune. While on the subject of Cameron—though I cannot in any way emulate Quentin Keynes—I would like to share one anecdote growing out of my experience searching for manuscripts.

In 1977, I had the great pleasure of being a fellow at the Institute for Advanced Studies in the Humanities at the University of Edinburgh, and one of the requirements of the fellowship was to give a public lecture. Mine was a wide-ranging talk on African exploration which mentioned Cameron only in passing. During the reception that followed the presentation, a gentleman asked if I would be interested in seeing a Cameron letter book. It so happened that two years before I had written on Cameron for the *Geographical Journal* in celebration of the centennial of his crossing Africa (he was the first explorer to cross the heart of the continent from east to west). In researching that article I expended considerable energy trying to find Cameron's missing African journals. One volume was at the Royal Geographical Society, with the other five supposedly in family hands. When the letter book was mentioned, it immediately dawned on me that here might be the needed link to the Cameron family, and such proved to be the case. The modern Camerons held not only the missing African journals but hundreds of letters covering his later African trips as well as all kinds of related memorabilia. Probably no such trove exists for Burton, but the experience suggests what a combination of persistence and good fortune can sometimes produce.

Dr. David Livingstone's papers, also at the National Library of Scotland, are full of references to Burton. Most of these focus on the Nile sources and controversy. My work in the papers of Grant, Cameron, and Livingstone suggests that there is much to be gleaned on Burton from the manuscript materials of his fellow explorers. Similarly, the kind of approach taken by the Livingstone Documentation Project could do much that is desperately needed on the subject of Burton.

Then there are all those unanswered questions. What were Burton's views, or lack thereof, on religion? Why were the Burtons childless? Was the true love of his life an Indian beauty? Did Burton really scorn the Victorian establishment, or is his bravado an attempt to hide insecurity? What is the explanation of his reluctance, especially in later life, to become close to other men? Did Burton, as he hints, intensely dislike his parents? Was he a scholar of the first magnitude or rather a prolific dabbler who loved delving into footnotes? What was the real nature of his differences with the Royal Geographical Society, with Christopher Rigby, and with others?

With these questions in mind, let us recapitulate some of the new perspectives that have been suggested by the speakers at this conference. Don Young, calling our attention to unpublished correspondence, urged that we need more, much more, work on Burton the geographer. He reminded us that Burton has been, to a very great degree, ignored by the most prestigious and longest-lived geographical society in the world, the Royal Geographical Society. Stephen Tabachnick and John Hayman both gave us admirable examples of the way in which close attention to Burton's writings may open up new worlds, and both directed our attention to key issues regarding Burton's views on race and empire. It might be added that Burton, though he may have had strong racial views, was not a racist in the traditional nineteenth- or twentieth-century sense. Nor, certainly, did he fit the standard mold of a flag-waving expansionist, carrying the Union Jack to the far outposts of the world. In particular, Professor Hayman brings us information on the inherent duality in Burton's persona, also illustrated in Sam Ingram's drawing, which shows Burton dueling against himself.

Guy Bishop has given us an account of a neglected episode in Burton's travels, the trip to Utah, and he shows that new sources await enterprising researchers. Quentin Keynes, in his own irresistible way, has shared with us the joys and the despairs of being a Burton collector and enthusiast. Burke Casari has afforded us a splendid example of what can be done by dogged, determined research. All of these speakers have opened our eyes to avenues that require further exploration.

The fact that Burton was a restless, in some ways rootless, immensely energetic, and curious man is of vital importance. We are here today because Burton was a wanderer. At least for posterity, that was not a curse but a blessing.